S. HRG. 114–130

RUSSIAN AGGRESSION IN EASTERN EUROPE: WHERE DOES PUTIN GO NEXT AFTER UKRAINE, GEORGIA, AND MOLDOVA?

HEARING

BEFORE THE

SUBCOMMITTEE ON EUROPE AND REGIONAL SECURITY COOPERATION

OF THE

COMMITTEE ON FOREIGN RELATIONS UNITED STATES SENATE

ONE HUNDRED FOURTEENTH CONGRESS

FIRST SESSION

MARCH 4, 2015

Printed for the use of the Committee on Foreign Relations

Available via the World Wide Web: http://www.gpo.gov/fdsys/

U.S. GOVERNMENT PUBLISHING OFFICE

97–882 PDF   WASHINGTON : 2015

For sale by the Superintendent of Documents, U.S. Government Publishing Office
Internet: bookstore.gpo.gov   Phone: toll free (866) 512–1800; DC area (202) 512–1800
Fax: (202) 512–2104   Mail: Stop IDCC, Washington, DC 20402–0001

(II)

CONTENTS

RUSSIAN AGRESSION IN EASTERN EUROPE: WHERE DOES PUTIN GO NEXT AFTER UKRAINE, GEORGIA, AND MOLDOVA?

WEDNESDAY, MARCH 4, 2015

U.S. SENATE,
SUBCOMMITTEE ON EUROPE AND REGIONAL
SECURITY COOPERATION,
COMMITTEE ON FOREIGN RELATIONS,
Washington, DC.

The subcommittee met, pursuant to notice, at 2:09 p.m., in room SD–419, Dirksen Senate Office Building, Hon. Ron Johnson (chairman of the subcommittee) presiding.

Present: Senators Johnson, Gardner, Shaheen, Murphy, and Kaine.

OPENING STATEMENT OF HON. RON JOHNSON, U.S. SENATOR FROM WISCONSIN

Senator JOHNSON. This hearing is called to order. I want to start off by thanking all the witnesses for taking the time, traveling here, and preparing some thoughtful testimony. I also want to offer my condolences to all of those who knew Boris Nemtsov, who considered him a friend and comrade. A real tragedy happened a day, I think, after we noticed this hearing. It certainly was not one of the things I wanted to talk about, certainly nothing we contemplated.

The purpose of this hearing is really to lay out a reality. It is to tell a story, and the story that needs to be told is what has become of Russia since Vladimir Putin has come to power. I am not going to tell the story. These gentlemen are going to be telling the story. Unless we understand the reality, unless we are willing to face the reality, unless we are willing to grapple with the reality, Vladimir Putin will continue his aggression, and it will not only destabilize Eastern Europe, it will destabilize the entire efforts of all those who want to seek peace and prosperity in the world.

We have a couple of photographs that I want to highlight. Starting to my right is a picture of Boris Nemtsov, a very courageous man that I had the privilege of meeting in my office, a man who brought to my office a longer list of people who needed to be added to the Magnitsky list. Unfortunately in the next picture right behind Senator Gardner is a picture of Boris Nemtsov having been assassinated with the Kremlin in the background. Now, that would be somewhat similar to an assassination carried out on Constitution Avenue with the Capitol in the background.

In my written opening statement, which I would ask to be entered into the record, we have laid out a timeline that starts with the fall of the Berlin Wall and then traces through the history. But in particular, I want people to pay attention to the history following the ascension of Mr. Putin to power in Russia. And I think probably the most powerful part of that timeline are the 29 assassinations of political figures, 29 assassinations and murders that have never been adequately solved. I think people need to really contemplate that.

Next picture, and we do not have the quote on there. This picture is actually a Ukrainian rebel talking about the number of Russian troops that he was thankful for that had entered Eastern Ukraine.

The next picture is one of tragedy, as Malaysian Flight Number MH17 was shot down out of the sky on July 17 of 2014. Two hundred and ninety-eight innocent civilians were murdered. This shows a picture of that. And then we have scenes of the devastation in Eastern Ukraine.

So that is a little pictorial history of the results of Vladimir Putin's aggression, and that is the story that needs to be told. That is the reality that needs to be faced.

[The prepared statement of Senator Johnson follows:]

PREPARED STATEMENT OF SENATOR RON JOHNSON

Good morning and welcome.

Today's hearing—the subcommittee's first hearing in the 114th Congress—is about documenting the history of Russian aggression in Ukraine and Eastern Europe and making sure that we, here in America, fully understand how dire the situation truly is. We need to face harsh reality and the fact that Ukraine needs our help in the form of defensive lethal military equipment, and it needs that help today.

In March 2014, with hardly any pushback from the West, Crimea was annexed by Russia. Prime Minister Yatsenyuk came to America last year asking for our help in his country's battle to ensure its territorial integrity. We should have immediately provided a minimal level of defensive lethal aid that Ukraine so desperately wanted. We should have taken it a step further by asking, "What else do you need?" America needed to show resolve then, and it desperately needs to show leadership and strength now, not only in Ukraine but around the world.

On December 5, 1994, the Budapest Memorandum was signed by Ukraine, Russia, the United States and the United Kingdom. In this agreement, Ukraine gave up the world's third-largest nuclear weapons stockpile in return for security assurances against threats or the use of force against its territorial integrity and political independence. Only 20 years later, Russia has blatantly broken its promise by brazenly violating the territorial integrity of Ukraine.

No one should be surprised by this behavior from Russian President Vladimir Putin. Under his leadership, Russian aggression against its neighbors has been building for years. The summarized timeline of Russia's destabilizing actions detailed below clearly demonstrates the threat Putin represents to neighboring democracies.

Date and Event

—Nov. 9, 1989: Berlin Wall falls.

—June 1991: Yeltsin wins first ever Russian presidential election.

—March 1997: Yeltsin appoints Boris Nemtsov first deputy Prime Minister.

—July 1998: Putin is appointed head of the Russian Federal Security Service (FSB).

—Nov. 20, 1998: Galina Starovoitova, a prominent liberal member of Russia's Parliament, is shot to death in her St. Petersburg apartment.

—Sept.-Oct. 1999: Putin sends Russian troops back into Chechnya in the wake of a series of bomb explosions in Russia which are blamed on Chechen extremists.

—Dec. 31, 1999: Yeltsin resigns, Putin becomes acting President.

—May 12, 2000: Igor Domnikov, a newspaper special-projects editor who reported on corruption in the Russian oil industry, is hit in the head and left lying unconscious in a pool of blood in his apartment building.

—July 26, 2000: Sergey Novikov, owner of an independent radio station that often criticized the provincial government, is shot four times in his apartment building in Smolensk

—Sept. 21, 2000: Iskandar Khatloni, a reporter for the Tajik-language service of Radio Free Europe/Radio Liberty, is attacked in his apartment by an ax-wielding assailant.

—Oct. 3, 2000: Sergey Ivanov, director of an independent television company, is shot five times in the head and chest in front of his apartment building.

—Nov. 21, 2000: Adam Tepsurgayev, a cameraman who covered the Chechen war, is shot dead.

—April 29, 2002: Valery Ivanov, editor-in-chief of a newspaper that exposed government corruption, is shot eight times in the head at point-blank range outside of his home.

—Aug. 21, 2002: Vladimir Golovlyov, a leader of the Liberal Russia faction in the lower house of Parliament, is shot dead in Moscow.

—April 17, 2003: Sergei Yushenkov, a member of the lower house of Russia's Parliament and an outspoken critic of Putin, is shot to death outside of his Moscow apartment.

—June 2003: Russian Government cites financial reasons for axing last remaining nationwide independent TV channel.

—July 3, 2003: Yuri Shchekochikhin, a vocal opposition journalist, dies after falling ill with a mysterious disease.

—June 19, 2004: Nikolai Girenko, a prominent human rights defender, is shot dead in his home in St. Petersburg.

—July 9, 2004: Paul Klebnikov, the first editor of Forbes magazine's Russian edition, is shot dead as he leaves his Moscow office.

—Sept. 14, 2006: Andrei Kozlov, the First Deputy Chairman of Russia's Central Bank who shut down banks accused of corruption, dies after he was shot outside of a Moscow sports arena.

—Oct. 7, 2006: Anna Politkovskaya, a journalist and fierce critic of the Kremlin, is shot and killed in her Moscow apartment building.

—Nov. 23, 2006: Alexander Litvinenko, a former KGB officer who was critical of Putin, died after being poisoned with radioactive polonium-210.

—March 2, 2007: Ivan Safronov, a journalist who embarrassed the country's military establishment with a series of exclusive stories, is found dead outside of his home.

—July 15, 2007: Marina Pisareva, deputy head of Bertelsmann AG's Russian publishinghouse, is found stabbed to death in her home west of Moscow.

—Aug. 2008: Russia invades Georgia; Medvedev signs an order recognizing the independence of South Ossetia and Abkhazia, the two breakaway regions in Georgia.

—Aug. 31, 2008: Magomed Yevloyev, owner of a popular news site that reported on human rights, dies from a gunshot wound to the head sustained while in police custody.

—Nov. 2008: Russian Parliament votes overwhelmingly in favor of a bill that would extend the next President's term of office from 4 to 6 years.

—Jan. 19, 2009: Stanslav Markelov, a human rights lawyer, and Anastasia Barburova, a young journalism student, are shot dead midday on a busy Moscow street.

—April 2009: Vyacheslav Yaroshenko, an editor at the newspaper Corruption and Crime, is beaten outside of his home; he passed away from his injuries weeks later.

—July 15, 2009: Natalia Estemirova, a prominent human rights journalist, is abducted from her home in Chechnya and shot dead.

—Nov. 16, 2009: Sergei Magnitsky, a lawyer who was jailed in revenge for his uncovering of massive tax fraud, dies in prison; Olga Kotovskaya, a TV journalist who critically reported on government leaders, dies after falling from a window.

—Dec. 15, 2011: Gadzhimurad Kamalov, founder and publisher of a Dagestani newspaper known for its editorial independence, is gunned down outside of his office.

—March 23, 2013: Boris Berezovsky, once the richest of the so-called oligarchs who dominated post-Soviet Russia and a close ally of Yeltsin who helped install Putin as President, is mysteriously found dead in his home outside of London.

—July 9, 2013: Akhmednabi Akhmednabiev, deputy chief editor of a Dagestani newspaper, dies after sustaining multiple gunshot wounds.

—Dec. 2013-Feb. 2014: Amidst large proreform protests in Ukraine, Putin offers to purchase $15 billion of Ukraine's debt and to reduce the price of Russian gas supplies to Ukraine. Violent protests flare, and by 2/22/2014 Yanukovych had fled Keiv.

—March 2014: President Putin signs a law formalizing Russia's takeover of Crimea from Ukraine.

—May 11, 2014: Pro-Russian separatists in Donetsk and Luhansk declare independence after unrecognized referendums.

—July 17, 2014: Malaysian flight MH17 is shot down and crashes near the town of Torez in Ukraine's Donetsk region; 298 people die.

—July 31, 2014: Timur Kuashev, a journalist critical of Russian policy in Ukraine, goes missing and is later found dead.

—Sept. 5, 2014: Ukraine and pro-Russian rebels sign a truce in Minsk.

—Nov. 5, 2014: Alexei Devotchenko, a popular Russian actor and opposition activist, dies in unclear circumstances.

—Jan. 24, 2015: Russian-backed rebels launch an offensive in Mariupol, Ukraine, killing 30 people and wounding 102 others.

—Feb. 11-12, 2015: Germany and France broker Minsk II cease-fire between Russia and Ukraine.

—Feb. 19, 2015: Ukrainian soldiers retreat from Debaltseve after 13 are killed and 157 wounded.

—Feb. 27, 2015: Boris Nemtsov, a prominent critic of Putin's war in Ukraine and a former Deputy Prime Minister under Yeltsin, is shot in the back four times by an unidentified attacker in a car as he crossed a bridge near the Kremlin.

Providing military equipment to Ukraine is not the only answer, but it is a necessary part of the answer. Ukraine needs economic and governance reforms, but those can succeed only in a peaceful and independent nation.

We all heard President Poroshenko address a joint session of Congress on September 18, 2014, and plainly state that his country needs more military equipment. ''Blankets and night-vision goggles are important,'' he said, ''but one cannot win a war with blankets.'' He went on to say, ''Just like Israel, Ukraine has the right to defend her territory—and it will do so, with all the courage of her heart and dedication of her soul!'' The Ukrainian people are willing to fight for their country. They just need a little help from their allies in America.

I look forward to hearing from our witnesses today on Russian aggression in Eastern Europe and learning how we can best support our allies in confronting this regional destabilization.

Thank you. I look forward to your testimony.

Again, I want to thank the witnesses, and I will turn it over to Senator Shaheen for her opening comments.

OPENING STATEMENT OF HON. JEANNE SHAHEEN, U.S. SENATOR FROM NEW HAMPSHIRE

Senator SHAHEEN. Thank you very much, Mr. Chairman, and thank you for your focus and work to bring this hearing together today. I want to echo your comments about the tragic killing of Boris Nemtsov. He was a tireless voice for all Russians and a firm believer in a bright future for the country. And even as we focus here on the Russian Federation's outward aggression, clearly we cannot ignore the repression that is happening inside Russia.

In the interest of time, I will submit my full statement for the record, and just want to end by welcoming all of our witnesses here today, and it is nice to have former President Saakashvili back with this committee today. And I look forward to hearing what all of you have to say and your thoughts about what more we can be doing to support the people of Ukraine.

Thank you.

[The prepared statement of Senator Shaheen follows:]

PREPARED STATEMENT OF SENATOR JEANNE SHAHEEN

Thank you, Chairman Johnson. I want to commend you for your focus and leadership on this critical foreign policy issue and for your work to bring this hearing together today before the Subcommittee on Europe. I also want to echo your comments about the tragic killing of Boris Nemtsov, who was a tireless voice for all Russians and a firm believer in a bright future for that country. Even as we focus here today on the Russia Federation's outward aggression, clearly, we cannot ignore the repression inside Russian today under President Putin. The Russian people and the world demand a transparent investigation into Mr. Nemtsov's murder and I sincerely hope we will see that. Russia's refusal to allow some foreign officials to attend his funeral was not a promising sign.

As the Chairman noted, we have five impressive witnesses here to help us better understand Russia's pattern of interference and aggression in Eastern Europe and think through appropriate responses. I join the chairman in thanking you for appearing here today.

Today, we see a Russian foreign policy that flouts international norms and responsibilities, a foreign policy that is based on political, economic, and even military intimidation and aggression. Airspace violations, disinformation and propaganda campaigns, energy corruption and trade restrictions are just a few of the tools used by Moscow.

Through Operation Atlantic Resolve and, the European Reassurance Initiative, the U.S. is already providing substantial support to our European partners, including Ukraine. That support should continue. In fact, it should be increased. We should consistently look for opportunities to assist our friends in Ukraine, Moldova, and Georgia, including helping them strengthen their political systems and economies through reform not for our benefit, but for the benefit of the people of those sovereign nations.

Congress, and particularly this committee, has played a critical role in this effort. Just last December, Congress passed the Ukraine Freedom Support Act, which authorized the President to provide defensive military assistance to Ukraine and tighten economic sanctions on Russia. I hope the administration will make use of these authorities.

I welcome your suggestions for what more we should be looking to do in Congress. Once again, thank you all for being here, and we look forward to hearing from each of you.

Senator JOHNSON. Thank you, Senator Shaheen. We do have a vote that is going to be called, and I believe that what is going to happen with that vote is we are going to be sitting in our chairs. So what we will do is when that vote is called, we all will leave. We will put this hearing into recess, and we will come back because I do not want anybody to miss the testimony.

But we will start off with President Saakashvili, former President of Georgia. He was the leader of Georgia from 2004 to 2013. Recently, he was appointed by Ukrainian President Poroshenko to serve as chairman of the International Advisory Council on Reforms of the President of Ukraine. President Saakashvili?

STATEMENT OF MIKHEIL SAAKASHVILI, FORMER PRESIDENT OF GEORGIA, AND CHAIRMAN, INTERNATIONAL ADVISORY COUNCIL ON REFORMS OF PRESIDENT OF UKRAINE, KIEV, UKRAINE

Mr. SAAKASHVILI. Thank you, Senator. Thank you, Senator Johnson, thank you, Senator Shaheen, thank you, Senator Gardner, for this wonderful initiative. I want to thank you, the committee and subcommittee, for the invitation. Perhaps it is a little unorthodox to find the former President representing the interests of another nation before the U.S. Senate, but I think the distinguished members of this committee understand why I have gone from being President of one nation to helping the President of another.

Ukraine and Georgia are on the front lines of the fight that may seem far away, but it is very much the fight that the American people and certainly the U.S. Congress understand more than anybody else in the world. This is not a fight about territory, about railway junctures, this or that town. This is a fight about principles, ideals, a way of life. This is a fight to determine whether we can escape from this curse of Soviet corrupt, cronyist, inefficient societies to being efficient democracies based on rule of law.

Ukraine, and here is the story of a Budapest memorandum, which I have to remind the members of the committee, Ukraine gave up 1,800 warheads, one-third of the Soviet nuclear arsenal, to help secure peace in post-cold-war Europe. That was on the insistence of United States. The United States, among other big powers, was the guarantor of Ukraine's territorial integrity and sovereignty and their statehood based on the Ukraine giving up their weapons.

Even more than that, on the insistence of this country and other great powers, the Ukraine has diminished its defense capabilities from having almost 1 million people serving in the military down to 120,000. Ukraine has neutralized the 120,000 tons of ammunition and mines. They have incapacitated 6,000 tanks for the last decades, and that was the time when they were complying with all their treaty obligations, while Russia was building up their military protection and propping up their muscles.

And now here we are. Ukraine has given all this up hoping that they will be guaranteed peaceful future. Certainly they were not planning to attack anybody. And instead of giving up several thousand nuclear warheads, they are asking basically for several thousand antitank missiles to defend themselves and to check Russian tanks deep into their territory, as well as some of their weapons. And certainly, supporting Ukraine at this moment means, first of all, in addition to all the other support, also giving them means to defend their democracy, and to support them building a viable, strong Ukrainian democracy. And I think it is now imperative to U.S. security and the world's security.

The old markers of Putin's reign are the gravestones of his critics and opponents. Every marker we can think of at this time is about increasing control of Russia or the Russian-speaking world. In September 1999, as director of FSB, Putin sent troops into Chechnya. Three months later he was Acting President of Russia. In August 2008 he invaded my country, Georgia. Three months later the constitution was changed to assure that when Putin returned to the Presidency, it would be a 6-year term. Putin's military excursions are always the prelude to the centralization of his personal power. This has made Russia more unpredictable and Europe and the United States less secure.

One year ago as the corrupt regime of Yanukovych fell, Russian forces moved into Crimea, then Ukraine, then there was downing of a passenger jet, as you rightly pointed out, Senator. In September of last year, President Poroshenko addressed the Joint Session of the Congress, and we are grateful for this opportunity. And he also asked that Ukraine requires defensive assistance because if not given that, Russia will continue to establish facts on the ground that will give them stronger position in the kabuki of future negotiations, and basically in the killing of Ukraine democracy. I think what Russia is up to is seizing the whole southern flank of Ukraine, seizing most of the east, and then going after the government in Kiev, and killing the very idea of Ukraine democracy.

After the war in 2008, a de facto ban on arms sales to Georgia was in place; as then, opponents were saying that providing Ukraine with lethal weapons would provoke Russia to escalate this conflict. But this appeasement ignores that Putin's aim is destabilize Ukrainian democracy. Adequate forces can stop aggression. In 1980, shoulder-fired Stinger missiles raised the cost to the Soviets in Afghanistan. That was the most decisive factor in the eventual defeat of the Soviet Army.

That is why it is very important that while there also Europeans who are doing the negotiations, the United States should take the lead empowering regional actors like Poland, and joining with forces with supportive nations like U.K. and the Baltics to create a coalition to help to arm and train the Ukrainian Army.

Ukraine must reform. I have focused on the case for arming Ukraine because without this there will not be a country to rebuild. But its success will equally be determined by fighting corruption, bringing the economy out of the shadows, increasing revenues to the state budget, and delivering better lives to the people of Ukraine. American support of all these efforts for the Ukrainian economy is critical, but time is short, and underneath the deception of the formation of war, the Russian plan is clear. They will seize more of the Ukraine. As I said, they will depose the government in Kiev if not checked in time. Only the swift and the immediate action of the United States Government to train and equip the Ukrainians can stop Putin's strategy to deconstruct the transatlantic architecture, to deconstruct the post-cold-war order.

America and the free world won Second World War, and Americans won the First World War, and they won the cold war. What we are seeing is a dramatic situation where all these gains might be reversed. Georgia is a small country, but when we were invaded in 2008, after the failed deal with the Europeans, it took the United States and many members of this very Congress to stop them by starting the humanitarian military operation, which did not involve sending U.S. boots on the ground, but certainly involved sending strong signals to the Russians that they should stop.

This war is much more complex than just war on the ground. This is a propaganda war. It is about controlling minds; and in this war we have yet to begin to fight back, to empower the Russian people to look at their own country and their own region, and to prevent encroachment of the Russian narrative into our politics and media. It was not just NATO army that saw the spread of communism. It was a collection of strong ideals with an army standing behind it. America, the origin of many of these ideals, was always further away from the front, and, thus, more able to resist the seeming appeal of realist moral compromise. The same must be true today. A democratic, secure Ukraine is the last nation between the revanchist Russia and America, and, overall, the free world.

Thank you, Senator, for hearing my testimony.

[The prepared statement of Mr. Saakashvili follows:]

PREPARED STATEMENT OF MIKHEIL SAAKASHVILI

Good afternoon. I want to thank the Foreign Relations Committee for the invitation to speak here today. Perhaps it is a bit unorthodox to find the President of one nation representing the interests of another before the United States Senate, but I think the distinguished members of this committee understand why I have gone from being a President to serving one.

Ukraine and Georgia are on the front lines of a fight that may seem far away from here. But Ukraine is what stands between America and Russian aggression. Ukraine earned its right to aspire to Western integration when it gave up over 1,800 warheads—one-third of the Soviet nuclear arsenal—to help secure peace in post-cold-war Europe. Twice since, the people of Ukraine have taken to the streets to defend this right. Supporting Ukraine—including by giving them the arms they need to fight for their future and by supporting their efforts to build a viable, strong, Ukrainian democracy and state—is now imperative to American security.

The road-markers of Putin's reign are the gravestones of his critics and opponents. His years in power can be measured by the rollback of federalization, rights, freedom, and opportunity. Every marker we can think of in his timeline is about increasing control of Russia and the Russian-speaking world.

In September 1999, as director of the FSB, Putin sent troops into Chechnya. Three months later he was Acting President of Russia. In August 2008, he invaded Georgia. Three months later the constitution was changed to ensure that when Putin returned to the Presidency, it would be for a 6-year term.

Putin's military excursions are always the prelude to the centralization of his personal power. This has made Russia more unpredictable, and Europe and the United States less secure in economic and military terms.

We don't know yet what will follow the invasion of Ukraine. One year ago, as the corrupt regime of President Yanukovich fell, Russian forces moved into Crimea. Moscow later announced the annexation of the peninsula. Russian military and intelligence operatives stirred up unrest in the Donbass region of Ukraine, which grew into a full-blown war including the participation of tens of thousands of Russian regular forces. Russian involvement increased after the downing of a Malaysian passenger jet by Russian air defenses that had been illegally brought into Ukraine in August 2014.

In September, President Poroshenko addressed a joint session of Congress with the request to provide Ukraine with defensive assistance. In bilateral talks with the U.S., Ukrainian officials have continuously submitted requests for assistance and defensive weapons. Ukraine has been provided some nonlethal assistance, including radars to help detect mortars, bulletproof vests, and some other basic aid and equipment.

But what will strengthen Ukrainian defense is lethal weapons—specifically, anti-tank weapons that can halt further Russian advance. When Russia knows there will be little cost to them to take the territory, they will take the territory. They will continue to establish facts on the ground that will give them a stronger position in the kabuki of future negotiations.

The arguments for withholding lethal aid are ones Georgia knows well: after the war in 2008, a de facto ban on arms sales to Georgia was in place. We couldn't even buy spare parts for our American rifles.

As then, opponents say that providing Ukraine with lethal weapons will provoke Russia to step up its military involvement and escalate the conflict. But this appeasement ignores that Putin's aim is to unseat the government in Kiev and fully destabilize Ukrainian democracy.

But adequate force can stop aggression: in the 1980s, shoulder-fired Stinger missiles raised the costs for the Soviets in Afghanistan so much that this was the single most decisive factor in the eventual defeat of the Soviet Army. As Putin's popularity soars post-Crimea, the one crack in his armor is the mounting, secret human cost of his war. To raise the cost for the Kremlin—on the front line and at home—further advances have to come with the fear of increased casualties.

The importance of maintaining a joint position with the Europeans is also cited frequently. But Ukraine has little reason, historic or contemporary, to hope for German support. The United States should take the lead, empowering regional actors like Poland and other neighbors of Ukraine, joining with supportive nations like the U.K. and the Baltics to create a coalition to arm and train the Ukrainian Army.

Ukraine must reform. I have focused today on the case for arming Ukraine because without this, there won't be a country to rebuild. But this is not to say its success will not be equally determined by fighting corruption, bringing the economy out of the shadows, increasing revenue to the state budget, and delivering better lives to the people of Ukraine.

American support of all those efforts, and support for the Ukrainian economy during the war, is critical. But time is short, and underneath the deception and the information war, the Russian plan could not be more transparent. They will seize more of the east and south of Ukraine; send defeated Ukrainian troops back to Kiev; and attempt to destabilize the social and economic situation enough that pressure mounts and the democratically elected President and Government of Ukraine collapse or are overthrown.

Only the swift and immediate action of the U.S. Government to train and equip the Ukrainians, as well as providing them with economic assistance, can stop Putin's strategy to deconstruct Europe, the transatlantic architecture, and transatlantic aspirations.

Putin is willing to fight in ways we are not. Georgia is a country of 4 million people—and Putin sent tens of thousands of troops to invade our country. Since 2008, Russia has spent well over a billion dollars propping up the budgets of Abkhazia and South Ossetia. In 2015, while the Russian state budget is being cut by 10 percent across the board, Russia's payments to South Ossetia have increased by 19 percent. Add to that the costs of military deployments to, and arrangements with, these regions. Add to that the costs of backing anti-European, xenophobic groups in Tbilisi to whittle away support for Euro-Atlantic integration under a government attempting rapprochement with an aggressive and bullying neighbor. Add to that the costs of the media and documentaries and reports Russia has funded to blame the 2008 war on Georgia and its NATO aspirations. The list goes on.

This is what Putin is willing to commit to ensure Georgia will not have a future that Russia does not dictate. He did this only to ensure that NATO could not offer Georgia a concrete pathway to membership. He did this so his narrative at home is secure.

And as Putin has made clear—Ukraine is a nearly divine cause for him. We understand only shadows of the billions of dollars he has spent to keep Ukraine in the "Russian world." According to U.N., over 6,000 people have been killed in the fighting in eastern Ukraine. Up to 20 percent of the industrial capacity of Ukraine has been removed or destroyed. A million people have been displaced.

In the past year, Russia has also backed political parties, heavy propaganda, and sharp economic pressure to erode support for Europe in Moldova, hoping to change the political landscape even before their territorial conquests in Ukraine bring the Russian Army closer to Moldova's door. And what Moldovans fear is that if Europe hasn't helped Ukraine—a far larger, richer, and more strategically important nation—Moldova will become a footnote of the regional conquest.

The price Putin is willing to pay, and to exact, is higher than we want to imagine.

In Georgia, in 2008, we fought because if we didn't fight for our sovereignty and our democracy and our independence, no one else ever would. It was, to be sure, an emotional choice—but also the rational one. We couldn't win a military war with Russia—but it is the ideological war that we believed needed to be fought, and won.

Fighting for our beliefs made many uncomfortable. Ukraine fights now for the same reason, and its Western friends are no less uncomfortable with their war. But make no mistake: Putin attacks Ukraine to weaken Europe, and to weaken NATO. When he makes the calculation that the time is right, he will cross the Article 5 line, probably in ways that are not expected. While we deliberate about definitions—Russian or Russian-backed, vacation or invasion—Putin will be fighting, and winning, an ideological war against the only force that has ever been able to contain and turn back expansionist Russian exceptionalism.

His war is a propaganda war. It is about controlling minds. And in that war, we have yet to begin to fight back to help empower the Russian people to look at their own country and their region—and to prevent the encroachment of the Russian narrative into our own politics and media.

It was not a NATO army that stopped the spread of communism. It was a collection of strong ideals with an army standing behind it. America, the origin of many of these ideals, was always further away from the front, and thus more able to resist the seeming appeal of realist moral compromise. The same must be true today. A democratic, secure Ukraine is the last nation between revanchist Russia and America.

Senator JOHNSON. Thank you, Mr. President. Do we have time?

VOICE. Votes just started.

Senator JOHNSON. Okay. We will recess at this point in time and hopefully be back in about 10 to 15 minutes. So, again, I apologize for that, but, again, this is an important hearing, and we are looking forward to your testimony.

Thank you. This hearing stands in recess.

[Recess.]

Senator JOHNSON. This hearing is called back to order. Our next witness will be Mr. Garry Kasparov. He is the chairman of the International Council of the Human Rights Foundation. Mr. Kasparov is a Russian pro-democracy leader, global human rights activist, author, and former world chess champion.

Mr. Kasparov.

STATEMENT OF GARRY KASPAROV, CHAIRMAN, HUMAN RIGHTS FOUNDATION, NEW YORK, NY

Mr. KASPAROV. My thanks to the subcommittee and to Senator Johnson for inviting me here today. It has been a very difficult last few days mourning the brutal murder of my long-time friend and colleague, Boris Nemtsov, in front of the Kremlin last Friday night, while also wanting to honor his memory and his fight by pressing the case for ending the regime of Vladimir Putin in Russia.

I have learned from painful experience that these first days after an atrocity are very important because people outside Russia quickly forget and move on. Boris was an outspoken critic of a police state that has no tolerance for critics. His imposing presence regularly embarrassed an increasingly totalitarian dictatorship that could not permit even the smallest amount of truth to leak out.

His latest report was to be on the presence of Russian troops in Ukraine, fighting Putin's war against a fragile democratic state in Europe. Boris also actively promoted the Magnitsky Act, a piece of rare bipartisan 2012 legislation that brought sanctions against Russian officials for not a brutal murder, but that of anticorruption attorney Sergei Magnitsky in 2009.

Boris Nemtsov was killed because he could be killed. Putin and his elites believe that after 15 years in power, there is nothing they cannot do, no line they cannot cross. Their sense of impunity, combined with an atmosphere of hatred and violence and Putin's propaganda, has created in Russia a lethal combination. Boris was not the first victim of this deadly mix. Georgia, Ukraine, and the stability of the modern world order is also under attack. Putin must justify his grip on power somehow. With his oil- and gas-based economy failing, he is following the path of Soviet dictators before him: propaganda, division, and war.

Enemies are needed so that Putin may protect Russians from them. Ukraine was always a tempting target, and the recent leaks have shown that an invasion plan existed even before the fall of Putin's puppet, Viktor Yanukovych. Inside Russia, independent journalists and opposition activists are portrayed as dangerous national traitors in language lifted directly from the Nazis.

Of course, I feel deeply the loss of my friend, Boris Nemtsov, and the prosecution of others who dare to speak against Putin. But it is Ukraine and what it illustrates about Putin and his regime that are more consequent to today's hearing. Since Putin took power in 2000, one Western administration after another declined to confront him on human rights at home or even his increasing belligerence abroad. The timeline of Russian repression circulated here today does an excellent job of listing many of the worse moments of Putin's crackdown. But there could also be a parallel timeline of all the meetings, deals, and smiling photo ops the leaders of the free world took with Putin while these atrocities were taking place.

The Western engagement policy that should have been abandoned as soon as Putin showed his true colors over a decade ago was continued at every turn, which emboldened Putin and delegitimized our opposition movement. Putin rebuilt the police state in Russia in full view of the outside world, and now he is confident enough of his power to attempt to export that police state abroad to Georgia, to Ukraine, to Moldova. Where next? He is testing NATO now, and he will test it further.

Putin also provides a role model for the rest of the world dictators and thugs by proudly defying the superior forces of the free world. From Iran to Syria to Venezuela, Putin's Russia provides both materiel support and what I would call amoral support.

Putin is not going away on his own. Ukraine is only his latest target. Ukraine must be defended, supported, and armed now. It may seem far away to you, but it is a front line of a war the United States and the rest of the free world is fighting whether it admits it or not. Sanctions are important, but it is obvious 6 months ago that they were not enough to deter Putin, and he must be deterred.

Stop treating Putin like any other leader who can be negotiated with in good faith. Stop legitimizing his brutal regime at the expense of the Russian people. The opposition movement Boris and I believed in and that Boris died for should also be openly supported, the way the West championed the Soviet dissidents. Let the people of Russia know that they have allies abroad the way Ronald Reagan told us—all of us behind the Iron Curtain that he knew it was our leaders, not us, who were his enemies.

Contrary to the widely circulated official polls, Putin does not enjoy broad public support in Russia, as was proved by hundreds of thousands of people mourning Boris in the street of Moscow. If you are truly popular, you can allow free media and free elections, and your critics are not gunned down in the streets. Putin's oligarch supporters must be forced to choose between giving him up and a doomed isolation. They cannot be allowed to continue to live like Trump and rule Stalin. The people of Russia want to be free, but defeating a globalized and energy-rich, heavily militarized dictatorship that has the tacit support of the free world is too much to ask.

You cannot negotiate with cancer. Like a cancer, Putin and his elites must be cut out. He must be isolated and removed, for only when Putin is gone can Russia be a free, strong, and independent country Boris Nemtsov always dreamed it could be.

Thank you.

[The prepared statement of Mr. Kasparov follows:]

PREPARED STATEMENT OF GARRY KASPAROV

My thanks to the subcommittee and to Senator Johnson for inviting me here today. It has been a very difficult last few days, mourning the brutal murder of my friend and colleague Boris Nemtsov in front of the Kremlin last Friday night, while also wanting to honor his memory and his fight by pressing the case for ending the regime of Vladimir Putin in Russia. I have learned from painful experience that these first days after an atrocity are very important, because people outside of Russia quickly forget and move on.

Boris was an outspoken critic of a police state that has no tolerance for critics. His imposing presence regularly embarrassed an increasingly totalitarian dictatorship that could not permit even the smallest amount of truth to leak out. His latest report was to be on the presence of Russian troops in Ukraine, fighting Putin's war against a fragile democratic state in Europe. Boris also actively promoted the Magnitsky Act, a piece of rare bipartisan 2012 legislation that brought sanctions against Russian officials for another brutal murder, that of anticorruption attorney Sergei Magnitsky in 2009.

Boris Nemtsov was killed because he could be killed. Putin and his elites believe that after 15 years of power there is nothing they cannot do, no line they cannot cross. Their sense of impunity, combined with the atmosphere of hatred and violence Putin's propaganda has created in Russia, is a lethal combination.

Boris was not the first victim of this deadly mix. Georgia, Ukraine, and the stability of the modern world order is also under attack. Putin must justify his grip on power somehow. With his oil and gas-based economy failing, he is following the path of so many dictators before him: propaganda, division, and war. Enemies are needed so that Putin may protect Russians from them. Ukraine was always a tempting target, and recent leaks have shown that an invasion plan existed even before the fall of Putin's puppet, Viktor Yanukovych. Inside Russia, independent journalists and opposition activists are portrayed as dangerous national traitors, in language lifted directly from the Nazis.

Of course I feel deeply the loss of my friend Boris Nemtsov and the persecution of others who dare to speak against Putin. But Ukraine and what it illustrates about Putin and his regime that are more consequent to today's hearing. Since Putin took power in 2000, one Western administration after another declined to confront him on human rights at home or over his increasing belligerence abroad. The timeline of Russian repression circulated here today does an excellent job of listing many of the worst moments of Putin's crackdown. But there could also be a parallel timeline of all the meetings, deals, and smiling photo-ops the leaders of the free world took with Putin while these atrocities were taking place. The Western engagement policy that should have been abandoned as soon as Putin showed his true colors over a decade ago was continued at every turn, which emboldened Putin and delegitimized our opposition movement.

Putin rebuilt a police state in Russia in full view of the outside world and now he is confident enough of his power to attempt to export that police state abroad. To Georgia, to Ukraine, to Moldova. Where next? He is testing NATO now and he will test it further. Putin also provides a role model for the rest of the world's dictators and thugs by proudly defying the superior forces of the free world. From Iran to Syria to Venezuela, Putin's Russia provides both material support and what I would call "amoral support."

Putin is not going away on his own. Ukraine is only his latest target. Ukraine must be defended, supported, and armed now. It may seem far away to you, but it is the front line of a war the United States and the rest of the free world is fighting whether it admits it or not. Sanctions are important, but it was obvious 6 months ago they were not enough to deter Putin, and he must be deterred.

Stop treating Putin like any other leader who can be negotiated with in good faith. Stop legitimizing his brutal regime at the expense of the Russian people. The opposition movement Boris and I believed in and that Boris died for should also be openly supported, the way the West championed the Soviet dissidents. Let the people of Russia know that they have allies abroad, the way Ronald Reagan told those of us behind the Iron Curtain that he knew it was our leaders, not us, who were his enemies. Contrary to the widely circulated official polls, Putin does not enjoy broad public support in Russia. If you are truly popular you can allow a free media and free elections—and your critics are not gunned down in the street.

Putin's oligarch supporters must be forced to choose between giving him up and a doomed isolation. They cannot be allowed to continue to live like Trump and rule like Stalin. The people of Russia want to be free, but defeating a globalized and energy-rich dictatorship that has the tacit support of the free world is too much to ask. You cannot negotiate with cancer. Like a cancer, Putin and his elites must be cut out. He must be isolated and removed, for only when Putin is gone can Russia be the free, strong, and independent country Boris Nemtsov always dreamed it could be.

Senator JOHNSON. Thank you, Mr. Kasparov.

Our next witness is Dr. Stephen Blank. He is a senior fellow for Russia at the American Foreign Policy Council. He is an internationally known expert on Russia and the former Soviet Union, and is the author of over 1,000 publications.

Dr. Blank.

STATEMENT OF STEPHEN BLANK, PH.D., SENIOR FELLOW, AMERICAN FOREIGN POLICY COUNCIL, WASHINGTON, DC

Dr. BLANK. Senator Johnson, it is a great honor to testify before your subcommittee with this exceptionally distinguished group of witnesses. Because my written statement deals with purely military issues, in my oral remarks I wish to talk about the broader strategic issues involved.

Russia's invasion and occupation of Ukraine represent the greatest threat to European security in a generation, the most naked case of aggression since Saddam Hussein invaded Kuwait in 1990, and arguably the most dangerous threat to international security and order today. It is the fruit of a long-developed plan whose origins can be traced back to 2005.

Russia has several objectives here. Many have already noticed that in keeping with the rhythms of Russian history, there is the belief that a little short victorious war can buttress the regime at home around a program of Russian imperialism and state nationalism. Further, it is an axiom of Russian foreign policy that none of the post-Soviet states, including those of Eastern Europe, really possess genuine sovereignty and territorial integrity. Therefore, the treaties guaranteeing that sovereignty and territorial integrity are merely scraps of paper.

This sentiment applies with particular force to Ukraine for it is clearly inconceivable to the Russian elite that Ukraine can follow a different trajectory than does Russia. Moreover, a Ukraine that looks westward is the greatest possible threat to the security of Putin's regime because it will infect Russia with the democratic virus. Indeed, the entire legitimacy of any Russian state is bound up with its being the true heir of Kievan Rus.

If Ukraine rebels against or rejects Russia's trajectory, then the entire legitimacy of the Russian state is called into question. This is especially the case because Putin and his team believe that empire is the only acceptable form of a Russian state, and Russia must, therefore, be an empire if his autocracy and kleptocracy are to be preserved. For all these reasons, a democratic revolution in Ukraine is anathema to Moscow and a pretext for an invasion.

Operationally, Moscow still intends to seize Mariupol, establish a land bridge to Crimea, and, if it could do so, establish as well as land bridge all the way to Moldova. Plans for this were already laid a year ago. Beyond destroying any possibility of an independent Ukraine, Moscow intends to overthrow the entire post-cold-war settlement of 1989 to 1991 in Europe and globally, and to do so by systematically applying the synchronized instruments of pressure we now know as so-called hybrid warfare. These policies predict more to any competent analyst, but unfortunately this administration and too many European governments do not take what happens in Russia seriously enough. Neither do these governments think Eastern Europe and the post-Soviet states are sufficiently important for us to have a real strategy regarding them.

This Russia-first strategy lies at the root of the continuing and shameful Western failure to understand or grapple with Russia and its aggressions seriously enough or to provide assistance to Ukraine as needed. As administration officials candidly admit, there is ''an asymmetry of will'' or of importance whereby Ukraine is supposedly more important to Moscow than it is to us or to European governments, and this inhibits us helping Ukraine as needed.

Indeed as reported on February 27 by the Wall Street Journal, the United States is slow rolling the provision of intelligence to Ukraine. Given the stakes involved for Ukraine, its neighbors, and partners, European and international security, this is an unacceptable policy. It undermines the credibility of NATO, of the United States, Europe, and beyond, and encourages aggression, and not only by Putin, and not only by Europe.

Therefore, the importance of these hearings should be clear to everyone, and I welcome the opportunity to testify before the committee today.

Thank you.

[The prepared statement of Dr. Blank follows:]

PREPARED STATEMENT OF DR. STEPHEN BLANK

Ukraine needs military help from abroad in terms of weapons, training, and finances to help sustain its government and economy in the face of Russian aggression. At a conference of the Potomac Institute, U.S. analysts and Ukrainian military leaders reported that the Ukrainian military continues to be severely disadvantaged by not being equipped with a list of the items that are becoming well known to those watching the current situation in eastern Ukraine: secure communications systems; antitank guided weapons with tandem warheads; counterbattery radars; UAVs for both reconnaissance and strike missions; and the ability to stream multiple intelligence sources into centralized command centers to get inside the ''decision loop'' of the Russian-backed forces.[1]

Therefore, Ukraine needs and has requested these capabilities, secure communications equipment, countermortar or counterbattery weapons, antiair, and antitank weapons and missiles. Ukraine also clearly needs UAVs or weapons to use against Russian drones. It also needs weapons to counter Russian artillery fire by the use of intelligence capabilities to determine the source and point of origin of those fires and then take them out. Ukraine also needs to devise an effective, democratic command and control structure that allows competent officers to rise to positions of responsible command, to train proficient officers whom men will follow and who understand modern warfare, and create a basis for integrating volunteers into a regular army commanded and led by proficient officers committed to democracy. In American terms it needs both an Edwin Stanton and a George Marshall. It also needs to sustain patriotic morale to counter manifestations of draft dodging and to demonstrate to the world that it is reforming. Right now it needs weapons as outlined above urgently as well as financial assistance and a long-term plan of both energy and financial assistance and steady support for (as well as pressure from outside) to reform its government and economy.

At the same time, there is little doubt that the White House and the NSC are holding up sending weapons to Ukraine at this point. But whatever their reasons are, there is little doubt that the Ukrainian Army will fight and with assistance can prevail over the rebels as long as Russia cannot operate freely there. Indeed, the fighting to date shows that only with substantial Russian help and the takeover of the operation by the Russian Army can the so-called rebels prevail in battle. If anything, this key fact justifies the provision of weapons and training to Ukraine as part of a broader strategy to wrest the strategic initiative away from Russia and give it to Ukraine and NATO.

The signs of this dependence on the Russian Army are evident everywhere. According to the IHS consultancy firm, Ukrainian authorities and the Potomac Institute, there are currently 14,400 Russian troops on Ukrainian territory backing up the 29,300 illegally armed formations of separatists in eastern Ukraine. These units are well equipped with the latest main battle tanks, armored personnel carriers and infantry fighting vehicles, plus hundreds of pieces of tube and rocket artillery. There are also 29,400 Russian troops in Crimea and 55,800 massed along the border with eastern Ukraine.[2]

—Russian units have made heavy use of electronic warfare (EW) and what appear to be high-power microwave (HPM) systems to jam not only the communications and reconnaissance assets of the Ukrainian Armed Forces but to also disable the surveillance unmanned aerial vehicles (UAVs) operated by cease-fire monitoring teams from the Organization for Security and Co-operation in Europe (OSCE). Russian EW teams have targeted the Schiebel Camcopter UAVs operated by the monitors and "melted the onboard electronics so that drones just fly around uncontrolled in circles before they crash to the ground," said one of the briefers at the conference. Russian EW, communications and other units central to their military operations are typically placed adjacent to kindergartens, hospitals, or apartment buildings so that Ukrainian units are unable to launch any strikes against them without causing unacceptable and horrific collateral casualties.

—The war against Ukraine is not a "new" strategy for Moscow; the Russian general staff has been preparing for Ukraine-type combat operations since 1999. Indeed, the Ukrainian operation has been planned by Moscow at least since 2005 and it is incomprehensible why the administration could not, or would not, formulate an assessment of what was happening in February 2014.[3] This speaks to our willingness and capability to assess Russian moves correctly and it is not encouraging.

—The Russian military's Zapad 2013 exercise (the word "Zapad" meaning "West" in Russian to denote that it was an operation designed to practice operations against NATO) was a dress-rehearsal for parts of the Ukraine campaign and future potential operations against the Baltic States. The exercise involved 76,300 total troops, 60 percent of which were drawn from the same Russian Interior Ministry (MVD) units that were used in the Chechen conflicts of the 1990s.

—Russia's information warfare campaign includes budgeting for the state-run Russia Today network (more than USD300 million per annum) and support for pro-Russian NGOs (USD100 million per annum).[4]

Russian casualties are much higher than imagined and reports of the true number of dead, wounded, POW and/or MIAs would undermine Putin at home. Second, Russian tactics are rather crude, essentially being massive artillery and air shelling of enemy positions. Such tactics mandate a traditional enormous output of ammunition and artillery. The numbers of shells being expended periodically forces Russia to accept truces in order to replenish its forces in Ukraine who are in full command of this operation. There are an estimated 17–20,000 Russian forces in Ukraine brought together or even cannibalized from many different Russian military units in order to bring ground, air, antiair, and support functions into the theatre. In addition, there is a substantial reinforcement of the naval, air, and missile forces in the Crimea, including nuclear-capable or so called dual use weapons being brought to Crimea.

We can learn the following lessons from this analysis. First, Putin cannot escalate the scale of conflict beyond present limits without antagonizing NATO further into a full-scale protracted war and he cannot afford that. He is also reputedly very afraid of media reports of the true extent of what evidently are sizable numbers of Russian casualties. For example, according to Ukrainian sources, at Debaltseve, 1,300 Ukrainians and 4,500 Russians were killed.[5] Why we are not publicizing Russian casualties escapes me. Third, there is every reason to believe that if NATO mobilized its resolve and capabilities to give Ukraine weapons and training as part of a comprehensive strategy that Ukraine's morale and capabilities would improve to the point of imposing much greater costs on Russia which is reaching the limit of its capabilities. Putin is already bringing troops form Central Asia and Siberia to Ukraine, indicating a manpower shortage and a lack of desire inside Russia to fight Ukraine. There are also many reports of disaffection within the Russian military. In other words, whereas NATO has hardly engaged, Russia is already feeling the pressure.

Russian tactics and strategy have aimed to keep the fighting at a level under NATO's "radar" to avoid a too protracted war. It appears Putin aims to create his "Novorossiia" and present the EU with a fait accompli by mid-year to persuade a divided Europe to remove sanctions and thus escape the risk of a protracted war. We have it within our power, if we can find the will to do so, not just to impose costs on Putin but to regain the overall strategic initiative and take it away for him by helping Ukraine to defend itself. What is needed here and in Europe and Kiev is a comprehensive strategy that embraces not only military but also strong economic and informational means to thwart this effort to sustain Putin at home, destroy an independent Ukrainian state, overturn the post cold war status quo in Europe, undermine European integration, and hasten the rupture of the transatlantic alliance. Our continuing passivity allows this shameful conquest and the spread of state terrorism and criminality orchestrated by Moscow and its subalterns in Crimea and Ukraine to spread with impunity. We must realize that this is the most naked aggression since Saddam Hussein invaded Kuwait in 1990 and respond accordingly to what is the greatest threat not just to European security but to international order. For if we do not do so, others will be even more emboldened by our inaction and confusion as we have seen with ISIL in the Levant and we can see with China in the South China Sea, and with Iran in regard to state-sponsored terrorism and nuclear proliferation. Continued passivity invites more escalation, and not only by Putin, whereas soundly conceived and implemented resistance upholds not only our values but even more importantly, our interests, both in Europe and across the globe.

End Notes

[1] Reuben F. Johnson, "Hybrid War Is Working," Jane's Defence Weekly, February 26, 2015.
[2] Ibid.
[3] Adam Entous, Julian E. Barnes, and Siobhan Gorman, "U.S. Scurries to Shore Up Spying on Russia," Wall Street Journal, March 24, 2014, www.wsjonline.com.
[4] Johnson.
[5] Conversations with Ukrainian officers and officials, Washington, DC, February 26, 2015.

Senator JOHNSON. Thank you, Dr. Blank.

Our next witness is Mr. Damon Wilson. He is executive vice president of the Atlantic Council. His areas of expertise include Central and Eastern Europe, NATO, and U.S. national security issues. From 2007 to 2009, Mr. Wilson served as special assistant to the President and senior director for European affairs at the National Security Council.

Mr. Wilson.

STATEMENT OF DAMON WILSON, EXECUTIVE VICE PRESIDENT, ATLANTIC COUNCIL, WASHINGTON, DC

Mr. WILSON. Chairman Johnson, Ranking Member Shaheen, and members of the committee, President Putin today poses a direct threat to American interests and values. His war in Ukraine aims to tear up the post-cold-war order and undermine American credibility. If we fail to stop Putin in Ukraine, we will face a series of conflicts and crises in the months and years to come.

At best, Putin may consolidate his autocratic grip at home and subjugate 75 million in Europe's East to a fate determined in Moscow. At worst, emboldened, Putin may be tempted to challenge a NATO ally directly. The choice we face, however, is not between fighting Russia or doing nothing. Rather, I believe doing nothing may lead to our fighting Russia. In this context, I would like to make five points.

This crisis began long before Crimea. Indeed, Russia's annexation of Crimea was the natural outcome of a clear, consistent policy dating back years. I detail this record in my full testimony. Second, Putin will not stop until he encounters serious pushback. Third, only the United States can galvanize Europe and the international community around an effective strategy to deter Putin for the long term. Fourth, any strategy should urgently and decisively back Ukraine, as well as other vulnerable states with significant economic and military assistance in the short term, while keeping the door open to the European Union or NATO. And fifth, we should neither abandon the Russian people nor the vision that a democratic Russia one day can find its peaceful place within a Europe whole and free.

Putin's strategy has been to use this crisis to consolidate his own hold at home through greater oppression of civil society and independent media even as he fuels nationalist fervor. He has created an environment of fear and intimidation fostering the circumstances that led to the assassination of Boris Nemtsov. Putin, of course, is also seeking to dominate his neighbors, to drain them of resources to fuel his kleptocracy, and to restore a sense of Russia's greatness in the only way a bully knows. He aims to prevent his neighbors from joining either NATO or the EU, achieving this through coercion when possible and by dismemberment and occupation when necessary.

Ultimately Putin knows that the best check on his power is a united transatlantic community, and he has sought to divide Europe, undermining the resolve for sustained sanctions. But the most tempting objective for Putin is to call into question the credibility of NATO's Article 5 mutual defense commitment as doing so would effectively end NATO.

A Russian move against an ally, such as a Baltic State, cannot be ruled out. Putin has demonstrated time and again that if he senses an opportunity to act he will, convinced that the West lacks the will or the ability to take decisive action. That is why today's situation is dangerous. We have seen repeatedly that Putin's objectives expand with success and contract with failure. This means that the best determinant of his action is Western action.

There is a tendency, however, to argue that the Europeans should take the lead on Ukraine. After all, we have our hands full with ISIS and other global responsibilities. But the Ukraine crisis is a Russia crisis, and Russia is too big, too strong, and too scary for Europe to resolve this without us. Without U.S. leadership, Europe may feel forced to accommodate a revanchist Russia, and we have seen throughout history this is a dangerous formula.

The United States has the ability to rally its allies and international partners around a comprehensive strategy that not only deters Putin's aggression, but avoids an unstable gray zone in Europe East. To do so, we should begin by articulating what we want to achieve. We should more decisively increase the cost to Russia, including by enacting sectorial sanctions and targeting Gazprom and Putin directly.

The most effective response is Ukraine succeeding and becoming a modern European state, and yet Western assistance to date is modest. There is no governmentwide concerted effort to assist Ukraine. There is no response commensurate with how we react to support campaigns like Ebola or ISIS. The United States is uniquely positioned to assist Ukraine to defend itself and to raise the cost of further Russian military action against Ukraine. Putin, after all, has lied to his own people about Russian forces fighting in Ukraine. But by reassuring Putin that we will either not provide or greatly constrain our military and intelligence assistance, we signal to the Kremlin what Russia can get away with.

Any assistance package should, therefore, be substantial, including antiarmor missiles, as well as intelligence support. Such a U.S. decision could unlock lethal military assistance from many of our allies. The U.S. Congress could also endorse a more substantial military presence along NATO's eastern flank, call for a halt to any further U.S. force withdrawals from Europe, and order a review of the U.S. force posture. Such a package could be designed to leverage U.S. commitment to European security to secure greater European commitments to defense investment.

We should respond to aggression in Europe's East by consolidating Europe's South. This would mean inviting Montenegro to join NATO and intensifying efforts to build United States strategic partnerships with Serbia and Cyprus. We should harness America's energy prowess to increase global supply while support European efforts to create a European energy union that includes Ukraine. And we should be explicit about our intention to negotiate a transatlantic trade and investment partnership that is open to Ukraine, Moldova, and Georgia.

As long as either KGB veterans retain their grip on the Kremlin or the nations in between NATO and Russia remain trapped in an insecure gray zone, we will face continued challenges and conflict.

Thank you.

[The prepared statement of Mr. Wilson follows:]

PREPARED STATEMENT OF DAMON M. WILSON

Chairman Johnson, Ranking Member Shaheen, members of the committee, President Putin today poses a direct threat to American interests and values. His war in Ukraine and his effort to sow division among our allies are aimed at tearing up the post-cold-war order and undermining American credibility and influence.

If we fail to stop Putin in Ukraine, we will face a series of conflicts and crises in the months and years to come.

At best, Putin may consolidate his autocratic grip at home and subjugate 75 million people in Europe's East to a fate determined in Moscow. At worst, an emboldened Putin may be tempted to challenge a NATO ally directly, hoping to deal a decisive blow to the alliance.

The choice we face, however, is not between fighting Russia or doing nothing. Rather, I believe doing nothing may lead to our fighting Russia.

We are better than that. The United States can take the lead in galvanizing the transatlantic community behind a comprehensive strategy, including ensuring that a well-functioning and well-armed European Ukraine emerges from this crisis.

In this context, I would like to make five points:

(1) Russia's war in Ukraine today is the natural outcome of Putin's policies in recent years (and the lessons he drew from our successive lack of responses).

(2) Putin will not stop until he encounters serious pushback.

(3) Only the United States can galvanize Europe and the international community around an effective, comprehensive strategy to deter Putin for the long term.

(4) Any strategy should urgently and decisively back Ukraine as well as other vulnerable states with significant economic and military assistance in the short term, while keeping the door open to the European Union (EU) or NATO for Ukraine, Georgia, and Moldova.

(5) We should neither abandon the Russian people nor the vision that a democratic Russia one day can find its peaceful place within a Europe whole and free.

This crisis began long before Crimea. Indeed, Russia's annexation of Crimea was the natural outcome of a clear, consistent policy dating back years. As confrontation replaced cooperation with the West as a source of legitimacy for the Kremlin, Russia meticulously laid the groundwork for what we are witnessing today. Former President Medvedev set out the doctrine of a "privileged sphere of interests." Putin articulated the "compatriots policy" in which Russia claimed the right to defend the interests of Russian speakers outside its borders, and it began distributing passports to strengthen its claims.

Russia undermined diplomatic efforts to resolve so-called frozen conflicts, and maintained Russian occupying forces as ''peacekeepers.'' At the last NATO—Russia summit in 2008, Putin ridiculed the idea of Ukraine as an independent state and questioned the status of Crimea in front of NATO leaders who had just failed to agree to begin preparing Ukraine for NATO. His creeping annexation of Georgia's breakaway regions prompted the Russian-Georgian War, consolidating his occupations. Russia both developed contingency plans and exercised seizing its neighbors' territory. Putin increasingly began wrapping all of his actions in a pseudo-ideology of Orthodox chauvinism.

He countered EU outreach with his own Eurasian Economic Union premised on coercion rather than attraction. Putin's intimidation tactics led Armenia first to abandon its EU association bid before forcing former Ukrainian President Yanukovych's about-face. Russia tried and failed to use economic coercion and energy threats to sway Moldova.

In the Ukraine crisis, Putin first probed with little green men to determine his freedom of maneuver in Crimea and, in the absence of resistance, brazenly seized the territory. The Kremlin then stoked the idea of a ''Russian Spring'' across southern and eastern Ukraine, creating the myth of Novorossiya and seeking to spark spontaneous revolts using ''political tourists'' from Russia. When that failed, Russia introduced Special Forces and intelligence operatives in Slavyansk, using the town as a base from which to seek to destabilize eastern Ukraine. And once Ukrainian forces gained their footing, nearly defeating the rebel forces, Russia opted for full-scale invasion. Today, the so-called separatists—former miners and farmers according to Putin—command greater quantities of the most advanced heavy weaponry than most European NATO nations.

While Ukraine is ground zero in the current struggle, there is no doubt that Putin's sights are firmly fixed on the two tiny nations that have dared stand up to his bullying: Moldova and Georgia. Moscow attempted to sway Moldova's recent elections with massive support for new pro-Kremlin parties, is courting separatists, and is poised to destabilize the nation. Despite Georgia's efforts to normalize relations with Moscow, Russia has continued its creeping annexation of Georgia's breakaway regions of Abkhazia and South Ossetia.

In the first instance, Putin has used this crisis to consolidate his own hold on at home, through greater repression of civil society and independent media even as he fuels a nationalist fervor. He has created an environment of fear and intimidation, at a minimum fostering the circumstances that led to the assassination of Boris Nemtsov. After all, the protests led by Nemtsov, much like the Maidan in Ukraine, pose a potentially existential threat to Putin's regime.

Putin, of course, is also seeking to dominate his neighbors, to drain them of resources to fuel his kleptocracy, and to restore a sense of Russia's greatness in the only way a bully knows—intimidating the weak, closest to him.

Furthermore, he aims to prevent any of his neighbors from joining either NATO or the EU, achieving this through coercion when possible and by dismemberment and occupation where necessary.

Ultimately, Putin knows that the best check on his power is a united transatlantic community. Hence, he has sought to divide Europe, undermining the resolve for sustained sanctions. But the most tempting objective for Putin is to call into question the credibility of NATO's Article 5 mutual defense commitment, as doing so would effectively end both NATO and America's role as a great European power.

A Russian move against an ally such as a Baltic State cannot be ruled out. Putin has demonstrated time and again that if he senses an opportunity to act, he will, convinced that the West lacks the will or ability to take decisive action. Debaltseve is only the latest case in point.

This is why today's situation is so dangerous. Putin will not stop and this crisis will not end until he encounters serious pushback.

We have seen repeatedly that Putin's objectives expand with success and contract with failure, or even the increased chance of failure. This means that the best determinant of his action is Western action.

There's a tendency, however, in Washington to argue that the Europeans should take the lead on Ukraine—after all we have our hands full with ISIS and other global responsibilities. This approach fails to understand that only the United States can galvanize Europe and other members of the international community around a tough-minded comprehensive strategy to deter Putin.

The Ukraine crisis is a Russia crisis after all. And Russia is too big, too strong, and too scary for Europe to resolve this without us. Germany may be a political and economic powerhouse, but Putin knows Chancellor Merkel cannot enforce European diplomacy. While the Chancellor has done a remarkable job in holding Europe together in this crisis, no European state can afford to get into a confrontation with Russia.

Without U.S. leadership in this crisis, Putin might succeed in creating a new dividing line in Europe. As he creates facts on the ground, he shifts the goalposts of what becomes an acceptable outcome in European diplomacy focused on ending violence. Europe may feel forced to accommodate a revanchist Russia rather than check its power. As we've seen throughout history, this is a dangerous formula.

Only U.S. leadership in this crisis provides the necessary condition to ensure the sustained resolve of our allies, most of who are bearing a far greater economic cost to their own economies.

Our strategy today is basically to raise the costs on Russia by imposing sanctions, protect NATO, and count on the long-term fundamentals, which are on our side and are working against Russia. The problem is that we have an immediate crisis. Putin likely sees the immediate future as his best window of opportunity. And in the short term, we may see a group of nations lose their sovereignty and Russia tempted to push further into NATO territory.

We can avoid this outcome. The United States has the ability to rally its allies and international partners around a comprehensive strategy that not only deters Putin's aggression, but also avoids an unstable grey zone in Europe's east.

To do so, we should begin by articulating our vision—what we want to achieve. I contend that should be a Europe whole, free, and at peace that embraces democratic nations in Europe's east and in which Russia can find its peaceful place in Europe.

We should more decisively increase the costs to Russia, including by refusing to treat Putin (and the FSB) as normal interlocutors, expanding the economic sanctions to include Putin and his inner circle, targeting Gazprom directly, and letting Moscow know that we are considering cutting off Russia from SWIFT financial transactions.

The most effective response is Ukraine succeeding in becoming a modern European state. We very well may see a shift from the military battlefields of the Donbas to the financial markets. Putin after all is out to win all of Ukraine, not simply consolidate his hold on a slice of territory in the east.

And yet U.S. and European assistance to date is modest. There is no government-wide concerted effort to assist Ukraine comparable to the White House-led effort to implement the reset with Russia. There is no response commensurate with how Congress reacted to support campaigns against Ebola and ISIS. The amounts of assistance under consideration are too small to serve as the catalyst for reform in a nation of over 50 million people. We are far more generous helping Jordan weather the Syria crisis as we plan to provide $1 billion in assistance to a nation of over 6 million. We provided $1 billion to 4.5 million Georgians after Russia's invasion. While the IMF and EU can and will contribute more to Ukraine, the U.S. sets the tone and for now the tone is ambivalent.

Assistance to Ukraine should include substantial military assistance. The United States is uniquely positioned to assist Ukraine to defend itself and to raise the costs of further Russian military action against Ukraine. There is no military solution in Ukraine and no one wants Ukraine to suffer a full-scale war with Russia. But by reassuring Putin that we will either not provide or greatly constrain our military and intelligence assistance, we signal to the Kremlin what Russia can get away with. Our current posture is escalatory as it gives Russia the confidence it needs to believe it can achieve particular means through military options at acceptable costs.

Any assistance package should therefore include substantial military assistance, including lethal military assistance such as antiarmor missiles, as well as intelligence support. Such a U.S. decision could unlock lethal military assistance from Canada and several other European and Asian allies. We should also support large-scale training in civil resistance in Ukraine as part of creating a deterrent state.

One vehicle for such assistance could be an expansion of the European Reassurance Initiative and renaming it the European Reinforcement Initiative to underscore its focus on building well-armed, well-trained deterrent states including frontline allies, key partners such as Finland and Sweden, and states under duress including Ukraine, Moldova, and Georgia.

Within NATO, even as we continue to implement the good Wales summit decisions, the alliance should also move away from ''reassurance,'' which focuses on the insecurities of our allies, and embrace ''deterrence,'' which underscores the threat. To this end, the U.S. Congress could endorse a more substantial U.S. and NATO military presence along NATO's Eastern flank until such time as Putin demonstrates that Russia is no longer a threat or potential threat to our allies; support a focused training effort to build frontline states' military capacities; call for a halt to any further U.S. force withdrawals from Europe; and order a review of U.S. force posture including how to prioritize Russia in determining the availability of forces to U.S. combatant commands. Such a package could be designed to leverage such U.S. commitments to European security to secure greater European commitments to defense investment.

Russia's aggressive new posture has translated into an intense diplomatic effort to buttress Russian influence elsewhere, especially in southeast Europe, and to disrupt ongoing European integration processes. We should respond to aggression in Europe's East by consolidating Europe's South. This would mean inviting Montenegro to join NATO, undertaking a renewed push to resolve the Macedonia name impasse, and intensifying efforts to build U.S. strategic partnerships with Serbia and Cyprus.

A comprehensive transatlantic strategy to deter Putin should expand the playing field to areas of strength for us—energy and trade. We should harness America's energy prowess to increase global supply, while supporting European efforts to create a European energy union that includes Ukraine and Moldova from that start. At the same time, we should be explicit that our intention is to negotiate a Transatlantic Trade and Investment Partnership (TTIP) that is open to European nations who have deep and comprehensive free trade agreements with the EU, notably Ukraine, Moldova, and Georgia.

At the same time, the United States must work much more closely with its allies on how to mitigate Russian efforts to sow dissension within the alliance. Such efforts begin with more transparency and stronger financial disclosure laws and practices in our societies to expose potential Russian manipulation of institutions, media, or political parties.

Western leaders must also assume responsibility for countering the Russian propaganda war by being willing to speak publicly and clearly about Russia's actions. If we are unable to recognize the threat Putin poses to our interests or challenge the misperceptions that surround this conflict, we are unlikely to formulate an effective, sustainable strategy sufficient to deter him for the long term—a strategy that is pursued not with confrontational rhetoric, but with resolve and determination.

As long as either KGB veterans retain their grip on the Kremlin or the nations in between NATO and Russia remain trapped in an insecure grey zone, we will face continued challenges and conflict. The Russian people, as we saw on the streets of Moscow Sunday, will some day have a say about their leaders. But the United States and its allies—along with Ukrainians, Moldovans, and Georgians—have a say about the latter.

Senator JOHNSON. Thank you, Mr. Wilson. Our final witness is the Honorable Steven Pifer. Am I pronouncing that correctly?

Ambassador PIFER. Yes, sir.

Senator JOHNSON. Good. Mr. Pifer is a senior fellow at the Brookings Institute and was a former U.S. Ambassador to Ukraine from 1998 to 2000. He is a retired Foreign Service officer with over 25 years at the State Department focused on United States relations with the former Soviet Union and Europe.

Mr. Pifer.

STATEMENT OF HON. STEVEN PIFER, DIRECTOR OF THE ARMS CONTROL AND NONPROLIFERATION INITIATIVE, THE BROOKINGS INSTITUTION, WASHINGTON, DC

Ambassador PIFER. Thank you, Mr. Chairman. Mr. Chairman, Senator Shaheen, Senator Gardner, thank you for the opportunity to testify today on Russia's aggression against Ukraine and the West's policy response. With your permission I will submit a written statement for the record and summarize it now.

What began as an internal Ukrainian political dispute became a conflict between Russia and Ukraine in early 2014. Moscow has used military force to seize Crimea, supported armed separatists, and sent regular Russian Army units into Eastern Ukraine. After a September cease-fire agreement failed, a second cease-fire, referred to Minsk II, was agreed to in February. That agreement is fragile at best. Its implementation will prove difficult.

Driving Russia's aggression has been a mix of geopolitical and domestic political considerations, including the fear that the Maidan demonstrations in Ukraine could provide a model that the Russian people might emulate. The Kremlin's goal appears to be to destabilize the Ukrainian Government and make it harder for Kiev to address its urgent economic reform agenda and draw closer to the European Union. The West has responded with sanctions. While having a major impact on the Russian economy, the sanctions have not yet achieved their political goal, to effect a change in the Kremlin's policy toward Ukraine.

Beyond Ukraine, the United States and Europe face a broader Russia problem. Moscow has operated its military forces in a provocative manner, and asserts a right to protect ethnic Russians and Russian speakers wherever they are located and whatever their citizenship. That could pose a threat to other states in the region, including Estonia and Latvia, both members of NATO.

In response, the United States and the West should pursue a multipronged strategy to deal with Russia's violations of Ukraine's sovereignty and territorial integrity and Moscow's generally more confrontational approach. That strategy should have five vectors.

First, NATO should bolster its ability to deter Russian threats to the alliance's members, particularly in the Baltic region. This entails enhancing NATO conventional force capabilities, including capabilities to deal with the hybrid war techniques that Russia has used in Ukraine.

Second, the West should support Ukraine, including through provision of substantial financial assistance if Kiev proceeds with serious economic reforms. If the Minsk II cease-fire by some chance holds and other terms of the agreement are implemented, but the Ukrainian economy collapses, that will hardly represent a success for Western policy.

Third, the West should maintain sanctions on Russia until Moscow demonstrates a full commitment to a negotiated settlement in eastern Ukraine and takes demonstrable and substantive measures to implement that settlement. Should Russia not do so, or should separatists and Russian forces resume military operations, the United States and European Union should rapidly move to impose additional sanctions. It is important to make clear to Russia that its egregious behavior will have significant costs so that the Kremlin does not come to believe it can pursue hybrid warfare elsewhere at a tolerable price.

Fourth, the United States should make preparations to provide increased military assistance to Ukraine, including defensive arms, particularly light antiarmor weapons. Provision of that assistance should proceed if the separatists or Russians violate the cease-fire, or if Moscow fails to implement the full terms of the Minsk II agreement. The assistance would fill gaps in the Ukrainian Army's ability to defend Ukraine against attack. The rationale is to enable the Ukrainian Army to impose costs on the Russian military, to deter Moscow from further fighting, and to encourage it to pursue a peaceful settlement.

Some express concern that U.S. provision of defensive arms would lead Russia to escalate, but escalation would carry major risks for Moscow. It would require more overt involvement by the Russian Army in eastern Ukraine. That would be more visible internationally, likely triggering additional sanctions, and to the Russian public, from whom the Kremlin has sought to hide the fact that Russian soldiers are fighting and dying in Ukraine. Others worry that providing arms would split U.S.-European unity. There is no evidence to back that. To be sure, Chancellor Merkel says that Germany will not provide arms, but during her visit in Washington on February 9, she did not give the President a red light or threaten a breakdown in transatlantic solidarity. And other allies would likely provide Ukraine defensive weapons once the United States began to do so.

Fifth, the United States should leave the door open for Russia to change course and help settle the conflict, even if expectations of such a change in Moscow's policy should be and are modest at best. Finally, while Ukraine has correctly deferred the issue of Crimea now, the West should continue to not recognize Russia's illegal annexation of the peninsula.

Mr. Chairman, Senator Shaheen, distinguished members of the subcommittee, Russia's actions on Ukraine and its more confrontational approach represent a serious challenge to the United States, Europe, and the West. Dealing with the Russian challenge requires a multipronged strategy based on firmness, patience, and solidarity with United States allies and friends in Europe. But given the large differences in economic, military, and soft power between the West and Russia, the West should be fully able to meet that challenge.

Thank you for your attention.

[The prepared statement of Mr. Pifer follows:]

PREPARED STATEMENT OF STEVEN PIFER

INTRODUCTION

Mr. Chairman, Senator Shaheen, distinguished members of the subcommittee, thank you for the opportunity to testify on Russia's aggression against Ukraine, and the U.S. and West's policy response.

What began as an internal Ukrainian political dispute became a Ukraine-Russia crisis in early 2014. Since then, Moscow has used military force to seize Crimea, supported armed separatists and ultimately sent regular Russian army units into eastern Ukraine. A cease-fire agreement was reached in Minsk last September, but the separatists and Russians failed to implement its terms. The Minsk II cease-fire agreed on February 12 may now be taking effect but seems fragile at best. Implementing other terms of the agreement will prove difficult.

Driving Russia's aggression has been a mix of geopolitical and domestic political considerations. The Kremlin's goal over the past year appears to have been to destabilize and distract the Ukrainian Government, in order keep that government from addressing its pressing economic, financial, and other challenges as well as from drawing closer to the European Union through implementation of the EU—Ukraine association agreement.

Beyond Ukraine, the United States and Europe face a broader Russia problem. Moscow has operated its military forces in a more provocative manner near NATO members and has asserted a right to ''protect'' ethnic Russians and Russian speakers wherever they are located and whatever their citizenship. That policy could pose a threat to other states, including Estonia and Latvia, both members of NATO.

The United States and the West should pursue a multipronged strategy to deal with Russia's violation of Ukraine's sovereignty and territorial integrity and Moscow's generally more confrontational approach. First, NATO should bolster its ability to deter Russian threats to the alliance's members, particularly in the Baltic region. This means enhancing NATO conventional force capabilities there, including capabilities to deal with the hybrid warfare techniques that Russia has demonstrated in Ukraine.

Second, the West should support Ukraine, including through provision of substantial financial assistance if Kiev proceeds with a serious reform agenda. Avoiding a financial collapse of Ukraine will require that the European Union and United States supplement the International Monetary Fund's extended fund facility program.

Third, the West should maintain economic and other sanctions on Russia until Moscow demonstrates a full commitment to a negotiated settlement in eastern Ukraine and takes demonstrable and substantive measures to implement that settlement. Should Russia not do so, or should separatist and Russian forces resume military operations, the United States and European Union should impose additional sanctions.

Fourth, the United States should make preparations to provide increased military assistance to Ukraine, including defensive weapons. Provision of that assistance should proceed if the separatists or Russians violate the cease-fire, or if Moscow fails to implement the terms of the Minsk II agreement.

Fifth, the West should leave the door open for Russia to change course and help end the conflict in eastern Ukraine, even if expectations of such a change in Moscow's course are modest at best.

Finally, while Ukraine has correctly deferred the issue of Crimea for now, the West should continue to not recognize Russia's illegal annexation of the peninsula. If Russian actions regarding eastern Ukraine merit sanctions relief, the United States and European Union nevertheless should maintain some sanctions, including measures specifically targeted at Crimea, until the peninsula's status is resolved to Kiev's satisfaction.

RUSSIA'S AGGRESSION AGAINST UKRAINE

Russia and the other independent states that emerged from the collapse of the Soviet Union in 1991 agreed to respect the state borders as they existed at the time. Unfortunately, Russia did not hold to that commitment. The Kremlin has supported separatist efforts and "frozen" conflicts in Transnistria, a breakaway part of Moldova, and South Ossetia and Abkhazia, breakaway regions from Georgia, whom Russia recognized as independent states following the August 2008 Georgia-Russia conflict. Moscow has again violated the sovereignty and territorial integrity of another state, this time, Ukraine.

Ukraine went through a wrenching internal political crisis from November 2013 to the end of February 2014, triggered by then-President Yanukovych's surprise decision not to sign an association agreement with the European Union. Following the security forces' use of deadly force against demonstrators in Kiev on February 19–20, Mr. Yanukovych signed a power-sharing agreement with the three main opposition party leaders.

Given public anger over the killings the two previous days, it is unlikely that the opposition leaders could have persuaded the demonstrators to accept the agreement. In any case, they had little chance. After signing the document, Mr. Yanukovych abandoned his post and disappeared, later turning up in Russia.

What had been an internal political crisis became a Ukraine-Russia conflict at the end of February 2014, when soldiers, in Russian combat fatigues without insignia, seized Crimea. The Ukrainians referred to them as "little green men." In a March 3 press conference, President Putin denied that they were Russian soldiers. Just weeks later, he publicly admitted that they were and awarded commendations to their commanders.

In April, armed separatists began to seize buildings in Donetsk and Luhansk in eastern Ukraine. Many were pro-Russian locals, but more "little green men" appeared. Moscow supported the separatists with funding, arms, and leadership. For example, last April, the self-proclaimed Prime Minister and Defense Minister of the so-called "Donetsk People's Republic" came from Russia and had apartments in Moscow. Further evidence that outsiders played a major role in the early days was the seizure of the opera house in Kharkiv, which they apparently mistook for the city administration building.

Over the course of the late spring and summer, as Ukrainian forces conducted a counteroffensive in Donetsk and Luhansk (also referred to as the Donbas), Russia provided the separatists with heavy arms, such as tanks, artillery, and surface-to-air missile systems. These apparently included the Buk (SA–11) surface-to-air missile that tragically shot down Malaysia Air flight 17 in July.

The Ukrainian military nevertheless made progress against the separatists during the summer, significantly reducing the amount of territory they held. On or about August 23, regular units of the Russia Army invaded Ukraine and attacked Ukrainian units in the Donbas. When a cease-fire agreement was worked out in Minsk on September 5, Ukrainian losses reportedly included between 50 and 70 percent of the armor the Ukrainian Army had deployed in the Donetsk and Luhansk regions.

Unfortunately, the September cease-fire never took full hold. The separatists and Russians did not implement key elements, such as the requirements for withdrawal of foreign forces and military equipment, or for securing the Ukraine-Russia border under observation by the Organization for Security and Cooperation in Europe. Instead, the Russian-backed separatists over the next 5 months took additional territory in eastern Ukraine, adding more than 500 square kilometers to what they had held on September 5.

Last month, with fighting escalating, German Chancellor Merkel and French President Hollande met with Ukrainian President Poroshenko and Russian President Putin in Minsk to seek a new settlement. After a marathon all-night negotiation, they announced a new agreement (Minsk II) providing for a cease-fire, withdrawal of heavy weapons away from the line of contact, and a series of steps to regulate the political and economic status of eastern Ukraine.

The terms of Minsk II are substantially worse for Kiev than the terms of the unfulfilled September 2014 agreement. Implementing the Minsk II agreement will require good faith and flexibility on all sides that has not been shown previously during this conflict. Many analysts expect the agreement to break down at some point.

It appears that Mr. Poroshenko agreed to Minsk II in the face of a deteriorating military situation and an urgent need for breathing space so that he could focus attention on a looming financial crisis and a very necessary economic reform agenda. Given Mr. Poroshenko's acceptance of Minsk II, Ukraine's supporters have little choice but to support the agreement and its implementation, however difficult its terms may appear.

Unfortunately, the separatist and Russian forces did not initially observe the cease-fire, which was supposed to begin on midnight on February 14. They attacked the Debaltseve salient occupied by Ukrainian Army units, which withdrew on February 18. The Ukrainians then reported ominous signs of preparations for a separatist/Russian attack on the large port city of Mariupol in southern Donetsk province.

Greater restraint was shown after February 25. While some shelling continues, the line of contact has been markedly quieter than it was during the first week of the cease-fire. The sides have pulled some heavy weapons back from the line of contact. The cease-fire, however, remains fragile and shaky, and Kiev remains concerned about possible preparations for an assault on Mariupol.

RUSSIAN MOTIVES

Russia today is passing through a difficult and dark phase, as evidenced by the tragic February 27 murder of opposition leader Boris Nemtsov, virtually on the doorstep of the Kremlin. Russia's goal with regard to Ukraine over the past year has been to destabilize and distract Mr. Poroshenko and his government. That makes it far more difficult for them to address the pressing economic, financial and reform agenda that confronts Kiev, including implementation of the reforms mandated by its program with the International Monetary Fund. It also makes it more difficult for Kiev to pursue implementation of the association agreement it signed last year with the European Union. Moscow seems to calculate that a new ''frozen conflict'' in eastern Ukraine—or perhaps a ''not so frozen conflict''—provides the mechanism to put pressure on Kiev.

This policy appears to be driven by a mix of geopolitical and domestic political considerations. Mr. Putin's concept of Russia as a great power includes a sphere of influence in the post-Soviet space. He does not seek to recreate the Soviet Union; the Russian economy does not wish to subsidize those of other states. But Moscow does want its neighbors to take account of and defer to its concerns, particularly as regards relationships with Western institutions such as NATO and the European Union.

Mr. Putin very much wanted Ukraine to join the Russian-led Eurasian Union, along with Belarus, Kazakhstan, and Armenia. Even under Mr. Yanukovych, however, Kiev made clear its preference for the European Union. If Moscow cannot have Ukraine in the Eurasian Union, it is working to hinder Ukraine's effort to draw closer to Europe.

Domestic political considerations factor heavily into the Kremlin's Ukraine policy. First, the two countries have long historical and cultural ties, and pulling Crimea and Ukraine back toward Russia plays well with Mr. Putin's conservative political base. That said, polls show that most Russians do not want the Russian Army fighting in Ukraine—which explains the extraordinary and sometimes disgraceful efforts taken by the Kremlin over the past 8 months to hide that fact from the Russian people.

A related consideration is the Kremlin's fear that the Maidan demonstrations that brought down Mr. Yanukovych might inspire Russians to mount large civil protests of their own. A weak Ukrainian Government incapable of meeting the challenges before it ensures that the Maidan model will have little attraction for the Russian populace. This consideration could mean that Mr. Putin wants a failed Ukrainian state. If so, that does not bode well for the prospects for the current cease-fire and Minsk II.

THE WEST AND A BROADER RUSSIA PROBLEM

Beyond Ukraine, the United States and Europe today face a broader Russia problem. As the Ukraine-Russia crisis intensified from March 2014 onward, NATO observed a significant increase in provocative behavior by Russian military forces, including nuclear exercises and snap conventional force alerts. NATO military authorities reported a marked jump in the number of cases of Russian bombers conducting flights near the air space of NATO member states.

Such behavior is of concern, as NATO and Russian military forces are increasingly operating in close proximity at a time of significant West-Russia tensions. That raises the prospect of accidents, miscalculation, or misunderstanding. For example, air traffic controllers in Scandinavia have reported two instances in which Russian intelligence-gathering aircraft recklessly switched off their radar transponders when operating in or near commercial air lanes.

Moscow has for some years asserted a right to "protect" ethnic Russians or Russian speakers wherever they are located and whatever their citizenship. Protecting ethnic Russians was a reason that Mr. Putin cited for seizing Crimea—once he admitted that the "little green men" there were in fact Russian soldiers. He made that claim even though there was no evidence of any threat to ethnic Russians on the peninsula.

One must question whether the Kremlin might seek to apply this self-proclaimed right elsewhere. Kazakhstan in Central Asia and Estonia and Latvia in the Baltic region have populations that are about one quarter ethnic Russian. The latter two states are members of NATO, to whom the United States has an obligation to defend under Article 5 of the 1949 Washington Treaty.

There may not be a significant likelihood of a Russian conventional attack on the Baltics or even of the appearance of "little green men" in Estonia or Latvia. But, given recent events and the Kremlin's hostile rhetoric, it would be prudent for NATO to assume that the probability of those contingencies is not zero and take appropriate measures.

Mr. Putin has displayed a deep antipathy toward NATO, for instance, in his March 18, 2014, speech on Crimea's annexation. Imagine a scenario in which 40–50 "little green men" seized a government building in Estonia, citing ethnic Russian grievances, while Moscow denied any connection. If Estonia asked NATO to treat that as an Article 5 contingency, and the alliance debated the issue for a week or two, that would be a major blow to confidence within NATO and a major victory for Mr. Putin. It is in NATO's interest to minimize the odds that the Kremlin might be tempted to try such a scenario.

THE U.S. AND THE WEST'S RESPONSE

The United States should respond to Russia's belligerence against Ukraine for three reasons. First, over the past 24 years, Ukraine has been a responsive partner when asked by the United States. In the early 1990s, largely at U.S. behest, Ukraine rid itself of the world's third-largest nuclear arsenal, including some 1,900 strategic nuclear warheads targeted or targetable on the American homeland. By 1996, Ukraine had transferred all the warheads to Russia for elimination. By 2001, it had eliminated the missile silos, intercontinental ballistic missiles and heavy bombers on its territory. In 2003, following the fall of Baghdad, Ukraine at U.S. request contributed three battalions to the Iraq stabilization force. For a period, the Ukrainian contingent was the fourth-largest in Iraq after the forces deployed by the United States, Britain, and Poland.

Second, the United States is a signatory, along with Britain and Russia, to the 1994 Budapest Memorandum on Security Assurances, which among other things committed those countries to respect the sovereignty, independence, and territorial integrity of Ukraine as well as to not use force or the threat of force against Ukraine. That was a key element of the arrangement that led to Kiev's decision to give up nuclear weapons. Russia has grossly violated its commitments under the memorandum. The United States should respond by supporting Ukraine and taking steps against Russia.

Third, Russia's use of force against Ukraine egregiously violates the cardinal rule of the European security order since the 1975 Helsinki Final Act: borders are inviolable, and states should not use force to alter them or take territory from other states. The West should push back against this, lest the Kremlin conclude that the kind of hybrid warfare that it has conducted against Ukraine is a successful tactic that could be applied at tolerable cost elsewhere.

Dealing with Russia's violation of Ukraine's sovereignty and territorial integrity and its generally more confrontational approach toward the West will require a multipronged Western strategy. That strategy should include measures to strengthen NATO, support Ukraine, and penalize Russia with the objective of getting the Kremlin to pursue and implement a negotiated settlement. Specifically, this means actions along five vectors.

STRENGTHENING NATO

NATO should strengthen its ability to deter Russian threats to the alliance's members, particularly by bolstering its defenses in the Baltic region and Central Europe. This entails prudent steps to enhance NATO conventional force capabilities, including capabilities to deal with Russian hybrid warfare techniques.

In order to assure Moscow that NATO enlargement would not entail the movement of significant military forces toward Russia's border, the alliance in 1997 said that there would be no "additional permanent stationing of substantial combat forces" on the territory of new NATO members. Although some allies have called for renouncing that policy in the aftermath of Russia's seizure of Crimea, the alliance as a whole has not agreed to a change. NATO has, however, begun strengthening its military capabilities in the Baltic States and Central Europe.

Beginning last April, the U.S. Army deployed light infantry units of about 150 personnel each in Poland and the three Baltic States. The Pentagon has described these as a "persistent" deployment: when a unit rotates out, another rotates in in its place. Other allies have increased the size and frequency of their ground force exercises in the region. The U.S. Army plans to deploy some 150 Abrams tanks and Bradley fighting vehicles in Europe, possibly in Poland; that would be sufficient to equip a heavy armored brigade.

The alliance's air presence for the Baltic air-policing mission has been increased substantially since last March. NATO now deploys on average at least three times the number of aircraft in the Baltics as it did previously. On the southeastern flank, U.S. and NATO warships make far more numerous entries into the Black Sea than before.

These actions have two principal goals. First, they aim to assure allies in the Baltic region and Central Europe of the firm alliance commitment to their defense. Second, they aim to make clear to Moscow that NATO will defend the territory of all allies.

Meeting in Wales last September, NATO leaders agreed to take additional measures. They decided to create a response force with the capability to deploy 5,000 troops anywhere within the alliance on 48 hours notice. In February, NATO Defense Ministers announced that headquarters elements would be established in the Baltic States, Poland, Romania, and Bulgaria. This step plus measures to enhance the infrastructure to support incoming troops and equipment will strengthen those countries' ability to receive reinforcements in a crisis.

Congress should support funds for these and other measures to strengthen the U.S. and NATO conventional force presence in the Baltic/Central European region. Specifically, the United States should consider increasing the size of its ground force presence in the region and seek the commitment of units from European allies to deploy on a "persistent" basis alongside U.S. units in the Baltic States and Poland. NATO should develop and exercise capabilities to deal rapidly with a "little green men" scenario on allied territory.

In overall conventional forces, the United States and NATO continue to enjoy qualitative and quantitative advantages over the Russian military. The Russian military, however, is engaged in a major modernization and rearmament program. NATO must make the investments needed to maintain its areas of advantage. The administration and Congress should urge allies to devote greater resources to the territorial defense of the alliance. Unfortunately, few allies currently meet NATO's agreed standard of spending 2 percent of GDP on defense.

The U.S. response should focus on strengthening conventional force capabilities. The U.S. Air Force reportedly maintains some 200 B61 nuclear gravity bombs at airfields in Belgium, Germany, Italy, the Netherlands, and Turkey. Those suffice to meet the mission of the U.S. nonstrategic nuclear arsenal in Europe, which is fundamentally political: to assure allies of the commitment of U.S. nuclear forces to their defense, and, if used, to signal the adversary to halt aggression or risk a strategic nuclear response.

Some have suggested that, in answer to Russian aggression in Ukraine, the United States should deploy nuclear weapons on the territory of NATO members in Central Europe, who have joined the alliance over the past 16 years. That would be unwise for three reasons.

First, deploying nuclear weapons to the relatively new members in the Baltic States or Central Europe would make the weapons more vulnerable to a Russian preemptive attack in a crisis. For example, the Iskander ballistic missiles reportedly deployed in Russia's Kaliningrad can carry conventional or nuclear weapons. From Kaliningrad, Iskander missiles could cover and rapidly strike targets in two-thirds of Poland and virtually all of Lithuania and Latvia. U.S. nuclear assets are far less vulnerable at their current bases.

Second, deploying nuclear weapons to the new members would violate NATO policy. Many, probably most, allies would oppose such a move. In 1997, the alliance stated that it had ''no intention, no plan and no reason'' to deploy nuclear arms on the territory of new member states. While some allies have sought to have NATO renounce or alter its policy of not permanently stationing substantial combat forces on the territory of new members, no ally has seriously raised the idea of changing the existing policy on no deployment of nuclear arms on the territory of new member states.

Third, placing U.S. nuclear weapons so close to Russia would be seen in Moscow as an extremely provocative act, on par with the attempt by the Soviet Union in 1962 to place nuclear-armed missiles in Cuba. It does not make sense to respond to Russian actions with a deployment that would make American nuclear weapons more vulnerable, cause a major rift within NATO, and unduly provoke Russia.

SUPPORTING UKRAINE FINANCIALLY

The United States and Europe should take substantial measures to support Ukraine with grants and low interest loans as it proceeds with difficult economic, rule of law and anticorruption reforms. The International Monetary Fund has reached preliminary agreement with Ukraine on a 4-year extended fund facility that will provide $17.5 billion. That will significantly help Ukraine, but it will not suffice. Ukraine could need an estimated $20–$25 billion more over the next 2 years in grants and low interest financing. Much of that will have to come from the European Union and United States.

EU officials and member states have shown no enthusiasm for providing assistance on that scale. But the European Union may well do more, as it does not wish to have to deal with a large failed Ukrainian economy on its eastern border. The United States also should be ready to contribute more than the loan guarantees promised for this year.

Finding this money on either side of the Atlantic will not be easy. However, if the European Union and United States are serious about helping Ukraine, they should provide the financial assistance. If the Minsk II cease-fire by some chance holds and other terms of the agreement are implemented but the Ukrainian economy collapses, that will hardly represent a success for Western policy.

Of course, the International Monetary Fund, European Union, and United States must, as a condition of their assistance, insist that Ukraine take the necessary reform steps. Absent such reforms, Western assistance would not go to good use. The leadership in Kiev hopefully understands that, unless they put in place the needed critical mass of reforms, the Ukrainian economy will remain mired in stagnation for years, if not decades.

PENALIZING RUSSIA

Over the past year, the United States, European Union, and other Western countries have imposed increasingly severe sanctions on Russia, following its seizure of Crimea and subsequent actions in eastern Ukraine, with the objective of effecting a change in Moscow's policy. The sanctions began with visa bans and asset freezes on selected individuals. They expanded to major sanctions targeting key Russian companies in the finance, defense, and energy sectors, for example, by barring new financing or the export of Western technology.

By all appearances, those sanctions are having a significant impact on the Russian economy, multiplied by the effect of the fall in the price of oil. For example, according to the Russian Central Bank, capital flight from Russia totaled $150 billion in 2014. Over the course of that year, Russian reserves fell from some $510 billion to $385 billion, in part due to an attempt to prop up the falling ruble; the ruble nevertheless has lost half of its value against the dollar since last summer. The Russian economy is officially projected to contract by 3 percent in 2015, while some economists predict a much steeper contraction. Russian officials have responded by seeking to cut most parts of the 2015 state budget by ten percent.

The sanctions, however, have not yet achieved their political objective, which is to get Russia to make a genuine change in policy course regarding Ukraine. If the cease-fire holds, that will be a positive step, but Moscow must also implement all of Minsk II's terms and use its significant influence with the separatists to achieve a durable settlement.

Should Russia not implement Minsk II, or should separatist or Russian forces resume military action, perhaps aimed at Mariupol, the United States and European Union should immediately apply new economic sanctions on Russia. U.S. and EU officials should consult now so that they have a package of additional sanctions ready.

Some analysts question whether the sanctions will prompt a different policy in Moscow. They argue that Mr. Putin will use the sanctions to blame the West for Russia's economic woes and rally the Russian people to resist. That has been his instinctive response.

If, however, the sanctions remain in place, Moscow's financial reserves will drop precipitously, and the average Russian will see a decline in his or her purchasing power. This could raise discontent among the Russian populace and affect Mr. Putin's approval ratings, something to which he pays close attention. Moreover, Mr. Putin almost certainly wishes to avoid exhausting Russia's reserves. It is not yet clear how he will respond if he faces this scenario.

In any event, even if one were not certain that sanctions would deliver the desired result, they allow the West to impose a significant cost on Russia commensurate with the nature of Russia's egregious actions in Ukraine. Absent sanctions, and having ruled out use of military force on Ukraine's behalf, the West would have few penalties of any real consequence to levy.

Mr. Putin may be betting that Western resolve to maintain the sanctions will flag, or that he can win sanctions relief with cosmetic gestures. A key date will be July, when some of the major EU sanctions, imposed last July, come up for renewal for another year. Maintaining Western solidarity and persuading the Kremlin that the sanctions will remain in place, or possibly increase, absent steps by Moscow to facilitate a settlement in eastern Ukraine, could prove critical to affecting the Kremlin's calculations.

U.S. sanctions to date have been imposed by Executive order, which allows the administration the flexibility to increase or relax them, depending on Russian actions. A threat of congressionally mandated (as opposed to authorized) sanctions could have a useful effect on Moscow. However, actually mandating congressional sanctions could well prove counterproductive.

The Russian experience has been that Congress is slow to remove sanctions, even when they achieve the desired Russian policy change. Moscow met the requirements of the 1974 Jackson-Vanik amendment in the mid-1990s, but Congress did not graduate Russia from the provisions of Jackson-Vanik and grant Russia permanent normal trade relations status until more than 15 years later, in December 2012—and then only in the Magnitsky Act, which leveled new sanctions on Russia. If Moscow believes that congressionally mandated sanctions will never be lifted, or if it believes that they will be lifted only years after Russia meets the sanctions' requirements, those sanctions give the Kremlin no incentive to change its policy.

ASSISTING UKRAINE MILITARILY

Over the past 10 months, the Ukrainian Army has had to face separatists equipped with large numbers of Russian heavy arms as well as regular Russian Army units. While the Ukrainian military has had some success, it is underfunded, undermanned and undertrained, and it faces an opponent that has better weapons and superior intelligence, surveillance and reconnaissance assets. The Ukrainian Army has significant gaps in capabilities that severely degrade its ability to defend Ukrainian territory against further attack by separatist and Russian forces.

The United States provided Ukraine $120 million in nonlethal military assistance in 2014, and the U.S. Army will this month begin a training program for Ukrainian National Guard units. The United States should do more.

Seven other former U.S. Government officials and I one month ago released a report entitled "Supporting Ukraine's Independence; Resisting Russian Aggression: What the United States and NATO Must Do" (http://www.brookings.edu/research/reports/2015/02/ukraine-independence-russian-aggression). In preparing the report, a number of us traveled in January to Brussels to meet NATO civilian and military leaders and to Ukraine, where we met with senior government and military officials, both in Kiev and at the Ukrainian army's field headquarters in Kramatorsk, in Donetsk province.

The report advocates a significant increase in U.S. military assistance to Ukraine—to $1 billion per year for 3 years. That is serious money; it reflects a serious effort to support the Ukrainian Army. While most of the recommended assistance would go to nonlethal equipment, the report also recommends a change in U.S. policy to allow provision of lethal defensive weapons.

In the nonlethal category, the report recommends providing counterbattery radars to pinpoint the origin of long-range artillery and rocket strikes, which the Ukrainians said cause 70 percent of their casualties. The report proposes provision of unmanned aerial vehicles for surveillance and reconnaissance purposes, electronic countermeasures to jam enemy unmanned aerial vehicles, secure communications equipment, armored Humvees and medical support equipment.

The report also recommends providing light anti-armor weapons. We were told in Kiev that the light antiarmor weapons in the Ukrainian Army's inventory are more than 20 years old, and a large number of them simply do not work.

Such assistance would help the Ukrainian military fill its gaps. The objective is not to give Ukraine the capability to defeat the Russian Army. That is beyond what a U.S. military assistance effort could do. The goal instead is to give the Ukrainian military the capability to inflict greater costs on the Russian Army should the Russians resume or escalate the fighting—and thereby deter Moscow from further military activity and encourage the Kremlin to work for a peaceful settlement.

Several concerns have been expressed about the proposal to provide Ukraine with defensive arms. One is that Russia will respond by escalating the conflict. The Ukrainians understand that risk and understand that they would bear the brunt of any escalation, yet they still request military assistance and defensive arms so that they can better defend their country.

Moreover, while the Kremlin might choose to escalate, that course carries risks for Moscow. Significant escalation would require more overt involvement by the Russian Army. That would be visible internationally and likely trigger additional sanctions, an area where the West has escalation dominance.

More overt escalation would also be visible to the Russian public, from whom the Kremlin has done everything that it could to hide the fact that Russian soldiers are fighting and dying in Ukraine. And taking additional territory means occupying land that will likely be more hostile to Russia, whose troops would face the prospect of partisan warfare. Escalation thus would not necessarily be an easy choice for the Kremlin.

Others worry that providing Ukraine defensive weapons would put the United States on the path to a direct confrontation with Russia. But there is nothing automatic or inexorable about that. The United States should not send combat troops to fight in Ukraine, nor should it provide advanced offensive weapons. The Ukrainians have asked for neither. To be sure, Washington needs to be clear with Kiev on the limits of U.S. military assistance, but the U.S. Government would control any decision about how far to go. It can build in significant firebreaks that would prevent a spiraling escalation.

Still others assert that a U.S. decision to provide defensive arms will cause a rupture in trans-Atlantic solidarity toward Russia. There is no evidence to suggest that. Our group was told at NATO that, if the United States provided defensive arms, other allies—such as Poland, the Baltic States, Canada, and Britain—might do so as well. During her February 9 visit to Washington, Chancellor Merkel said that Germany did not favor providing weapons but did not suggest that a U.S. decision to do so would cause a split with Europe. While she did not give President Obama a green light on this question, she had every opportunity to give him a red light—but she did not do that.

Our report and recommendations were issued before the Minsk II cease-fire agreement was concluded on February 12. The President may have put off a decision regarding additional military assistance and defensive arms to see whether Ms. Merkel's mediation efforts could succeed. The cease-fire did not get off to a good start but appears after February 25 to be taking better hold. Given Ukrainian concerns about Mariupol, it bears a close watch.

It nevertheless would make sense for the administration and Congress to proceed with preparations for providing Ukraine greater military assistance and defensive arms, first by agreeing on the necessary authorities and legislation. Doing that will take time. Should the cease-fire break down and major fighting resume—unfortunately, not an unlikely prospect—early preparations would facilitate earlier delivery of assistance to Ukraine. U.S. preparations to provide assistance and defensive arms might even bolster the cease-fire, as the prospect of fighting a more capable Ukrainian military could affect the calculation in Moscow of the costs and benefits of resumed military action.

Should the cease-fire take full hold and the separatists and Russians proceed in good faith to implement the other elements of the Minsk II agreement, a decision could always be taken later to suspend the actual delivery of defensive arms.

LEAVING THE DOOR OPEN FOR A CHANGED POLICY IN MOSCOW

The U.S. administration and other Western countries have talked of leaving Russia a "diplomatic off-ramp"—a way out of the current crisis. Securing a settlement with Russian agreement is important, as any settlement that provides for genuine peace and a degree of normalcy needs Moscow's buy-in. Russia has many levers, including military and economic, to destabilize Ukraine. Unfortunately, it is not yet clear that the Kremlin is prepared to consent to such a settlement.

More broadly, Moscow's assault on Ukraine has brought U.S.-Russian and West-Russian relations to their lowest point since the end of the cold war. Whereas Western policy toward Russia in the 1990s and early 2000s was based on an assumption that Moscow wanted to integrate into the West and was prepared to abide by a rules-based European security order, it is clear that neither premise now holds.

This is not a desirable state of affairs. There remain issues on which U.S. and Russian interests converge—such as preventing Iran from acquiring a nuclear weapon, supporting the Afghan Government, and implementing the New START Treaty. Cooperation makes sense on these questions. The downturn in relations, whose onset predates the Ukraine crisis, makes cooperation in other areas more difficult at present.

The West should leave the door open for a better relationship with Moscow if the Kremlin changes the policies that have triggered and deepened the current crisis—even if expectations of a change in Russian policy are modest at best. More broadly, the West should, while pushing back against Russian actions in Ukraine, make clear that a restoration of a more positive general relationship is possible if Russia shows that it is ready to again abide by rules that served European security well for almost four decades.

DO NOT FORGET CRIMEA

The Ukrainian Government has correctly focused its attention on resolving the conflict in eastern Ukraine and said that the issue of Crimea should be addressed in the longer term. That is a wise course, especially as it is difficult to see how Kiev can muster the leverage in the near term to restore Crimea's status as part of Ukraine.

While Crimea is not now the priority issue, it is important that the United States and the West not forget or move to "normalize" the question. Until such time as the status of the peninsula is resolved to Kiev's satisfaction, the international community should sustain a policy of not recognizing Crimea's illegal incorporation into Russia.

If Russian actions regarding eastern Ukraine merit some sanctions relief, the United States and European Union nevertheless should maintain sanctions on Russia, pending a satisfactory settlement on Crimea's status. These would include sanctions that, among other things, prevent trade with, investment in and international air routes to Crimea.

CONCLUSION

Mr. Chairman, Senator Shaheen, distinguished members of the subcommittee, Russia's actions in Ukraine and its more confrontational approach present a serious challenge to the United States, Europe, and the West. Dealing with that challenge requires a multipronged strategy that aims to bolster NATO and support Ukraine while taking steps to constrain Moscow's possibilities to threaten other parts of Europe.

Getting this strategy right will require firmness, patience, and solidarity with U.S. allies and friends in Europe. Doing so will be difficult, no doubt. But given the significant differences in economic, military, and soft power between the West and Russia, the West should be fully able to meet this challenge.

Senator JOHNSON. Thank you, Ambassador Pifer. I would like to start my questioning with President Saakashvili. You obviously have firsthand experience with Russian aggression. Can you just describe the events of August 2008 and what prompted Vladimir Putin to stop advancing into Georgia?

Mr. SAAKASHVILI. Yes, Senator. What happened in 2008 was that we were invaded by a full-blown Russian force, which involved more than 100,000 ground troops. More than 1,000 armor, 200 combat planes on the Russian side took part in the operation against basically what was a very small-sized Georgian professional army. And in that respect, first we had mediation—exactly the kind of mediation that you see now with Presidents Hollande and Merkel by President Sarkozy.

And he came in. We signed the cease-fire agreement. Georgian Army withdrew its forces from the contested area, the invaded area, and Russia was supposed to withdraw as well. Instead, Russian after several days said the situation on the ground has changed. They no longer would abide by the agreement and started toward the capital. And what really had stopped back then was the United States proclaiming military humanitarian operation, moving the 6th Fleet first to the Georgian ports, and putting planes in Romanian base, and putting the airbase in Turkey on high military alert, and basically starting to patrolling skies close to Georgia.

The other day I was at the office of Senator Kirk, who told me that he was—back then I did not know this story. He was on duty in Patagon. Actually, the United States had to bring back, based on our agreement because we were the second biggest—then first biggest big capita contributor to operation contributors to Iraq and Afghanistan, but at that moment it was Iraq. But the agreement we had, the standby agreement with President of the United States was that we could repatriate our troops.

So, what happened that the United States—the United States told—first Russia told the United States to remove the military cargo plane from the tarmac of Tbilisi International Airport. The United States refused to do that, and that was already a first important signal because they were told they were going to bomb the Tbilisi International Airport, and they did not want to move American plane. American plane stayed on the tarmac, and that spared us at least that bombing.

And second thing, they had to bring back Georgian brigades, and Georgian skies were fully under control of Russian military jets, and they told me that they would not let through the United States plane. And then the Pentagon and Senator Kirk told me he called specifically the Russian Defense Minister and said we are coming anyway. This is the U.S. plane, and you do not ever dare to touch us. And they came in, and they did not do it. And that was the key moment when after this launch of military humanitarian operations just few miles away from our capital. Vladimir Putin's clearly proclaimed goal to depose democratic elected Government of Georgia, just like they have, I think, more or less proclaimed goal to the post-government in Ukraine.

They had to stop, and that was a clear sign that stepping up and counting on who would blink first, Putin at that moment blinked first. And I have to say I believe there is no—they will try to depose government of Ukraine. They will not succeed to do it, but that is clearly their plan. It is not their plan to just hold to those two regions like it was never planned to hold just the regions of Georgia. They wanted to get rid of Georgian democracy because that was a dangerous precedent. Exactly like having Ukraine succeed, it would just be a very dangerous precedent for Russia.

So sometimes like in Western Berlin, Americans protected West Berlin even from Stalin and Western allies, and they protected it through all the decades of the cold war. And West Berlin was a showcase of what democracy looks like—should look like. And that really convinced all of us—I mean, we did not need much of convincing. But they convinced, overall, the nations that they had to revolt against the Communist system. Exactly the same type for today's world like Georgia was in 2008, I think Ukraine is West Berlin of today, and it is much more protectable than West Berlin ever was, and even more protected than Georgia was, by the way, because Georgia did not have that strategic depth. That is what the example of Georgia clearly shows.

Senator JOHNSON. Thank you, Mr. President. Mr. Kasparov, we hear frequently that we are trying to offer off ramps to Vladimir Putin. Do you believe Vladimir Putin is looking for any off ramps whatsoever?

Mr. KASPAROV. Well, he is looking for—of course he is looking for any negotiation because he is very successful using them for his own purpose, but he has no interest in any settlement. I believe for long time that his interest was opposite to the interest of United States and the free world because he always wanted to create conflicts. He needed conflicts in the Middle East. You know, conflict was the Iranian nuclear problem because these conflicts helped to push oil prices up, and that was actually crucial for his regime.

And now, he needs conflicts because that is the only way for him to sell his dictatorship in Russia. The Russian propaganda machine is probably worse now than at any time of, you know, that I can remember. My mother tells me that—she is turning 78—that it is probably worse than Stalin because it is more powerful. We have 24/7 propaganda that is anti-American, anti-Semitic, anti-Ukrainian, and everybody. And this atmosphere, you know, helps Putin to keep Russian subdued.

His goal, as was mentioned in two testimonies here, is not even just to take over the territory of neighboring countries, though of course he would love to enlarge Russia. But most importantly, to destroy the system of international security that has been created in Europe since 1945 and 1991 at the end of the cold war. So that is why all these negotiations for him are just, you know, a way to buy time, and to gain some more ground, and to move forward because Putin does not ask why. He always asks why not, and if the free world vacates a space, Putin grabs it.

Senator JOHNSON. Thank you. You know, we have all heard of the little green men. Do any of the witnesses have any kind of intelligence estimates in terms of what Russia has committed to

Eastern Ukraine, how many troops, what type of equipment? Well, let me go to Dr. Blank.

Dr. BLANK. In my written testimony, I quote an article from Jane's, which came out the other day, was based on conferences between Ukrainian officers and American analysts. They say there are 14 to 20,000 Russian troops. A report in today's paper said that NATO estimates or that the Pentagon estimated 12,000. So I think we would be comfortable saying between 12 and 20,000 Russian troops—20,000 Russian troops are in Ukraine, thousands more on the border. And a large-scale naval and air buildup, including the deployment of nuclear capable missiles, is taking place in Crimea as we sit.

Senator JOHNSON. President Saakashvili.

Mr. SAAKASHVILI. Yes, I have photos, Senator, and this clearly shows these are the weapons that are only given to Russian special forces. This is highly sophisticated Russian weapons, would never been given to any local rebels. They have brand new infantry fighting vehicles that have an artillery launching system. We hear that they were spotted in parades inside Russia just 1 year before the invasion, obviously, so that is the regular equipment of the Russian Army.

But besides, I mean, what we have to keep in mind here, first, this is the war as you rightly said, Ambassador Pifer, that Russia does not even recognize as fighting. So first, they were sending in non-Caucasians, mostly Muslim population with the hope that mainstream Russians would not really care if they die. Now, they are mostly sending troops from beyond the Euros, Far East, mostly from—many of them from ethnic minority areas from there, and basically are very careful not to send in Moscovites and St. Petersburg people. They had to send them airborne in August of last year, and there was a political scandal after it became known that a number of them died, and that really spread in Russia.

So what this is telling you, that once you raise the cost for Putin's invasion, there is no way he is going to pull up with the stakes because there is a very thin layer of tolerance Russians have toward human casualties. That is the structure of his troops, clearly indicate to you that he is really in some way here has very little maneuver. So that is so important to take this decision on the weapons because that is going to reverse many of the plans he has about that country.

Senator JOHNSON. Thank you.

Senator Shaheen.

Senator SHAHEEN. Thank you, Mr. Chairman. Ambassador Pifer, I understand that you and a number of your colleagues have recently released a report on the Ukrainian crisis. And one of the cases that you make in that report is the importance of providing military assistance to Ukraine, including defensive lethal weapons and light antiarmor weapons. Can you tell this panel more about the case that you make in that report and why you believe this is important?

Ambassador PIFER. Thank you very much, Senator. This was a report that was issued by the Atlantic Council, Brookings, and the Chicago Council on Global Affairs by seven other former government officials and myself. Five of us went to NATO and went to

Ukraine in January to get an understanding of the military situation in eastern Ukraine and also specific needs. And, most importantly, we had a retired American four-star, General Chuck Wald, with us who really could apply a military mind.

The recommendations that we made were for serious assistance, we proposed a billion a year for 3 years. And we looked at what the Ukrainians both in Kiev, but we also went out to the field headquarters at Kramatorsk and met with the commander there, the sorts of requests that they had. Actually most of their requests were for nonlethal assistance. They wanted things like counterbattery radars that could pinpoint the origin of rocket strikes and artillery 20 to 40 kilometers out. We were told that 70 percent of Ukrainian casualties are from rocket and artillery strikes. They wanted reconnaissance unmanned aerial vehicles. They wanted the means to jam Russian and separatist drones. They wanted secure communications.

The one item that they requested in terms of lethal military assistance was light antiarmor weapons. We were told in Kiev that basically their stockpile of these weapons are at least 20-plus years old, and about three-quarters of them just do not work. So that was the one item that they thought there would be a very useful American contribution to filling a significant gap that they have.

Senator SHAHEEN. And, Mr. Wilson, since the Atlantic Council was part of that report, can I ask you to comment on that, as well as respond to the concerns that have been raised by Germany and France about the potential for escalation of the situation in Ukraine if we provide defensive weapons?

Mr. WILSON. Yes, Senator Shaheen. Thank you very much. I think of it in two respects. Strategically, if we are trying to help support the Ukrainians in achieving a better political outcome for this crisis in the East, the absence and the clarity of the fact that we actually will not provide them weapons actually undermines their hand at the negotiating table. So if you do believe in a political resolution to what is happening in the East, by strengthening the Ukrainian's ability to raise the cost for Russians if they turn to further violence, it actually puts President Poroshenko in a much better position in negotiating an outcome, some type of outcome.

But there is also a moral argument that we should think about, and that Ukraine is a sovereign independent nation that is under attack from a neighbor. It is under attack from a neighbor after recognizing that we were a party through the Budapest Memorandum to helping to respect and preserve its territorial integrity. So I think there is a moral aspect to this as well, that Ukraine has an essential right to be able to defend itself, and us standing back and not supporting it in that effort I think carries a heavy strategic and moral burden.

We have heard from some of our European allies of concerns about potential for escalation. The Russians could double down and escalate more. It is hard for me to see how—President Putin is already arguing to the Russian people that the United States and other allies are sending weapons to Ukraine. He has already demonstrated his willingness to frontally invade Ukraine if he needs to. It is hard for me to see how this measure actually is any more provocative than what he is doing in Ukraine today.

There is concern that this will split the alliance. What is important is that we do this in a way that brings many allies on board with us. I think Ambassador Pifer has said that there are at least six allies in Europe and Asia, Canada as well, that would likely join the United States decision if it were a clear decision.

There is nervousness about a somewhat ambivalent U.S. decision to do this lightly, partially. But I think a serious strategic decision to stand by Ukraine with support at the level that this report recommends would demonstrate to our allies that this was a serious strategy, and we would have some of them stand with us, and others not openly opposed.

Senator SHAHEEN. And do you have any insights into at what point, if at all, Germany and France might change their view about the importance of providing weapons?

Mr. WILSON. I think the greatest likelihood is first United Kingdom, Denmark, Poland, Lithuania, Romania, Canada, Australia, a collection of countries that would stand with us first. I do not think you are likely to see, certainly on the German side, active participation in the supply of lethal military equipment. However, at the Wales summit, Chancellor Merkel and President Hollande did commit, as part of the NATO commitment, to intensify NATO's support for Ukrainian defense modernization.

And so I think there is a way not to exclude them, but actually to include them in a broader strategic effort to stand by Ukraine's building of its defense capacities. They likely would not be coming around on the provision of lethal military assistance, but they certainly would be partners, I think, in a broader effort.

Senator SHAHEEN. So you do not see that if Russia continues to violate this Minsk II agreement and continues to provide material and people, that might encourage Chancellor Merkel and President Hollande to change their view? Does anybody—I mean, you are about to tell me that you do not think so, I assume.

Mr. WILSON. Well, I would not completely rule it out. You have seen a remarkable evolution of Chancellor Merkel's position on this. The incredible nature of what President Putin is doing has actually turned German public opinion against Russia, which was not something that you could have imagined. And frankly, Chancellor Merkel has been the key to holding European unity together on the sanctions.

I think this would be quite a big step for them to move to providing lethal military assistance to Ukraine. However, you have seen the Germans step forward this year in providing lethal military assistance to the peshmerga in Iraq, which in and of itself is a significant development in German defense policy.

Senator SHAHEEN. And does everybody else on the panel agree with that? Dr. Blank?

Dr. BLANK. Well, the French Foreign Minister said the other day that if Russia continues to break the agreement reached in Minsk, that France will vote to expand sanctions. I think Russia will continue to violate the Minsk Accords, and, therefore, I expect France to follow what President Obama did today, which is to extend sanctions and perhaps even enlarge them. And I suspect that if Russia does continue to move forward, that the French can be persuaded over time to support the provision of lethal weapons. Germany I am less certain of for the same reasons that Damon has given.

Mr. SAAKASHVILI. Well, on France, I remember that in 2008 when they supplied the Mistral helicopter warships to Russia, when we strongly protested to them because they were guarantors of the cease-fire. Some very high level French officials replied to us rather cynically that they would supply us with the missiles to sink Mistrals, no problem with that. We would like to buy them. So France could be very inventive in this kind of an approach.

Now, in Germany, I saw Chancellor Merkel last month at the European People's Party Summit in Brussels. And actually she took the floor initially and she told, I know some people at this table want to ease the sanctions. I am telling you out right, Germany will not support it. And, certainly, she leads the sanctions movement right now.

I do not see Germany, for a number of very historic and psychologic reasons, ever supplying lethal equipment, but they have been good on supplying nonlethal—I mean, in some other cases. I think that might happen. But I do not think that should be an impediment to the United States doing that because, as I said, I mean, there is a moment when only the——but the problem with not supplying weapon is of different sort. Right now, and this was the case in the case of Georgia, because there is no signal from Washington, Czechs, Slovaks, Bulgarians, and number of others are refusing to provide even spare parts for all Soviet equipment to Ukraine precisely for the reason because they do not want to stand alone if Washington is not on board. So Washington by not supplying the lethal weapons is also blocking the others from doing it because that has really become this cornerstone right now, and we are at the crossroads. And it is really becoming very counterproductive.

And finally on sanctions. Now, sanctions are always helpful, but there is a moment after which a sanctions-only policy can cause lots of risk because what might happen is that Putin might think, ''I have very little time left, and I had better seize the rest of it, go for it. And then, of course, from the position of strength negotiate my way out of sanctions because Europeans will not sanction anybody for a long time. After some time they will come back to me.'' So there is a moment when if there are only sanctions, those sanctions might be not as helpful as before because you need something else.

Senator SHAHEEN. Thank you. My time is up.

Senator JOHNSON. Senator Gardner.

Senator GARDNER. Thank you, Mr. Chairman, and thank you to the witnesses who are here today. I think it was shortly after the demise of the Soviet Union that President H.W. Bush had said, ''Europe: whole, free, and at peace.'' And now we see the complete rearrangement attempts by Russia to rearrange the post-cold-war world international order.

We have seen a determined effort by brave soldiers in Ukraine to stand strong, fight valiantly, but obviously overwhelmed and over matched. We have seen questions in the Baltic States about our commitment. You and I, President Saakashvili, had a conversation about timing, promises made, and concern within the region, concern about the promises that the United States has made, morale within Ukraine, questions as to the resolve of NATO or whether NATO could withstand a challenge, if that is indeed the question before us.

And so, your experience in Georgia, you talked to the chairman a little bit about your experience in Georgia. Mr. Wilson talked a little bit about the commitment of the international community. As President Poroshenko's advisor, as the person who has taken this role on internationally, do you believe that the international coalition exists and will stand with the United States to step up our efforts?

Mr. SAAKASHVILI. Well, Senator, you are absolutely right. There was U.S. guarantee, first of all, for Budapest Memorandum. But, you know, one of the things I omitted to mention was that U.S. also—the Ukraine also gave, on U.S. insistence, MANPADS. They do not have even MANPADS because the United States strongly insisted they follow up on their promise not only on nuclear warheads, but they also gave thousands of MANPADS, which they now really need in that situation.

So, yes, on international coalition, certainly I agree with Mr. Wilson. There are countries that are very much on board, but they are right now—basically they are standing by because they want for Washington to lead. There is no way they can do something on their own. I still would imagine Poland might risk doing something on their own, but for the others, I would not bet on that. But once there is a signal coming from Washington, I am sure there will be strong coalition also on supplying weapons.

And one thing we should know also. There are number of people, nationals from these countries, including my nation, that are fighting as volunteers on the side of Ukrainian army. We have Georgian officers dying for them there. You know, we are proud that we are part of the operations, ISAF and the others. We had lots of people that died in Afghanistan and Iraq, fighting alongside of the Americans.

But also now, many of those people—many of the people that went to Afghanistan with Americans, went to Iraq, they are fighting in Ukraine. I have seen—we have a couple of hundred Georgians from those operations that also went through the training, now fighting there. You also see Poles there. You see countries from people from Baltic countries.

So there is already coalition of citizens of the nations around Ukraine fighting for Ukraine because they understand that it is also their battle. There is also lots of sympathy in those nations, but for that, you need for those countries to get together. You need empowerment from Washington. And I am sure there are countries that will be American allies on military front. Nobody is asking for American boots on the ground. That is out of question. Ukraine has enough fighting manpower. They have people who will stand up for their nation. But also—and there will be other countries that will be a kind of second rank, like Germany, that might not be part of the large-scale military efforts. But they are certainly an important component of the sanctions.

So I think there is an overwhelming sympathy toward Ukraine, and I do not see this falling apart unless something dramatic comes from Washington.

Senator GARDNER. Ambassador Pifer, you mentioned in your testimony that the sanctions had not yet achieved their political goal. And you also then followed it up with we need to make it clear to Russia that its actions will have a cost. So I want to talk about what do you envision—what would indeed extract that political goal, and what would the cost be to Russia—needs to be reached?

Ambassador PIFER. Well, I believe that if the West can maintain unity on sanctions, the key point here is persuading Moscow that the sanctions will remain in place until the Russians change their policy course. You have already seen significant damage to the Russian economy—$150 billion in capital flight from Russia in 2014. Russian reserves fell by about $140 billion over the course of the year, largely to support the ruble, and it was not very successful. The ruble is about 50 percent of the value against the dollar that it was last summer.

So there has been a huge impact on the Russian economy. In fact, the Russian Finance Minister, who about 3 weeks ago recommended cutting every aspect of the Russian state budget by 10 percent, except for defense, is now saying they have to cut defense. So there is an impact here.

But I think Mr. Putin is playing—he is making a bet, and that bet is that the West will not be able to sustain the sanctions. And there is a very key date here in July, which is the European Union imposed sanctions for a 1-year duration. EU practices are that if the goal of the sanctions is not achieved, the sanctions are rolled over. They are extended for another year. Mr. Putin, I think, is hoping that there will be enough opposition among EU countries in July that those sanctions will not be extended, and that he can basically escape the economic pain without having to do the desired course correction.

I think that if, in fact, the West can sustain those sanctions and make it clear they are on through the end of the year into 2016 until there is a policy change, he is going to see his reserves probably run out within 1½ years or so, and he is going to see the average Russian facing huge inflation. I think 19 percent is the current figure, and the possibility that their average purchasing power may decline 15 to 20 percent over the course of the year. That, I think, is going to have an impact on Mr. Putin and his policy.

Senator GARDNER. And, Dr. Blank, in your written statement and in your testimony, how much time would we need in Ukraine for proper training with equipment from the United States?

Dr. BLANK. Well, that would depend on the nature of the specific equipment, but I do not think it is really going to take that long. Everything we have seen says that the Ukrainians learn very quickly how to use the equipment. If we send it over and we send over enough people who know how to use it and train, I think it would be a matter of days or weeks at the most.

But I have to argue that we should have been doing this months ago because, like Ambassador Pifer, I believe that Putin is going to try to use the spring and summer to create a fait accompli in Ukraine and break up the sanctions regime on that basis.

Senator GARDNER. And that is another question I want to ask. How much time do you think we have on this?

Dr. BLANK. Not much because, frankly, my sources have told me that basically the Pentagon has been told to go slow on giving even the equipment that it has. There is no excuse for saying that we are still doing a review of Ukraine needs. This has been going on for a year, yet it is going on. So I think there are people in the administration who are deliberately undermining efforts to help Ukraine, and they need to be stopped and the signal sent out that we will help Ukraine as needed.

Mr. SAAKASHVILI. Senator, last year, last March, when the whole thing started, had already started, I have been telling some of the administration officials why do you not target this training, you know. There is framework for training. They told me we do not have enough time. Now, Russia has done since then six or seven rounds of training of the so-called separatist troops. What it indicates to lots of time has been lost. We know from Georgian experience, Americans are very good at training. You put marines or some other troops on the ground, they can train full brigade within 4 or 4 weeks.

Remember, the other point for U.S. training is that you do not have this kind of disorganized troops when you have U.S. trained soldiers that might be used for all kind of bad means, like, you know, either moving against legitimate government. When you have a U.S. element present, that also brings lots of stability to constitutional systems of democracies. That is one of the beauties of U.S. training.

And Ukraine also needs this kind of stability as badly as it needs help with defending itself, because you know Russian plan is, you know, to inflict defeat on Ukrainians. That is their hope. And then send back disorganized troops to do some nasty things back in Kiev. And that will never work if U.S. training is already installed and in place.

I already have a list that Ukrainian Government has submitted to the United States, which is really quite a need, and that list has been circulated quite a lot. The U.S. Government knows what is needed. It has been done after lot of consultation with unofficial ones, with people in Pentagon.

This is very important, and by the way, I think it is very modest. I looked at the list. It looks really modest. It includes also some antitank TOW javelin missiles, but really the numbers are so modest. And in terms of money, it is really not much. What is really expensive, Ukrainians have antiair, they have heavy artillery, they have lots of other things. It is not matter of money. It is matter of political will right now.

Senator GARDNER. Thank you, Mr. Chairman.

Senator JOHNSON. Senator Murphy.

Senator MURPHY. Thank you very much, Mr. Chairman. Thank you to all of you for being here today. I am supportive of extending defensive weapons to the Ukrainian Army, but I want to express now some questions regarding some reservations that I have about that position, but then just open with a comment regarding my frustration on this conversation.

We are obsessed with this question of providing arms to the Ukrainians, and it matters. But it is obsessive within the American context because it is one of the few, if only, tools that we have to try to blunt and combat Russian aggression in the region. I was there at the height of the Maidan protests. I spent 2 hours sitting, talking to President Yanukovych and listening to him give a litany of perceived and real abuses that Europe and the United States had perpetuated against Ukraine.

And the reality is that we had a long time to try to stop this from becoming a crisis, but because we are not resourced as a nation, because we hamstring ourselves when it comes to the tools that we could use to try to create greater partnerships with countries that are at risk of falling into the growing Russian sphere, we then are stuck with crises in which we know how to respond to because we know we have the ability to supply weapons.

And so, in the fall I was in Belgrade on the day that Putin was coming into town to do an unprecedented display of military prowess through the central streets while our Ambassador was begging for a few thousand dollars from the Federal Government here to increase exchange programs with the United States, right? We are not doing what is necessary in and around the region to try to stop these crises from happening in the first place.

And so, I think this is an incredibly important conversation, and I am glad that we are having this hearing. But we had better adopt a strategy soon to stop the next Ukraine from happening so that we are not caught in this crisis, which is a hard one to unwind.

Here are the reservations that I have. First, let us admit that what we are talking about would be relatively unprecedented. We are talking about the overt arming of a country that is under military threat and occupation and invasion from the Russians. Let us just acknowledge that during the cold war when the Soviets were a much bigger threat to the United States than the Russians are today, we did not do this, whether it was the invasion of Hungary or the invasion of Afghanistan. Well, we used other tools. We did not at that time make the choice to provide overt arms to the Afghans or the Hungarians. I think the circumstances are different today, and so I am supportive of defensive weapons. But this is not a no-brainer. This would be a change in the policy that we have traditionally observed over the long course of the last 100 years.

Here are my two reservations, and I will ask the first question to Mr. Pifer. Your report and all of your recommendations are predicated on the belief that the cost will be so high to Putin that he will change behavior. Whether or not this provokes him or not, what if the cost is not high enough? What if he continues to move forward and the first round of arms that we supply are not enough? What are you recommending? Are you recommending one batch of defensive weapons? Are you recommending that we stage our supply line to them to respond to the moves that the Russians make? What is our endgame? When is enough too much?

Ambassador PIFER. Senator, I think that is a very good question, and let me break my answer down into two pieces. First of all, we believe that providing these levels of weapons, which I think are actually on the low end of the military scale—we are not talking about F–16s, advanced offensive weapons, and we are certainly not talking about American combat troops. But the calculation here is that when you go and you look at what the Russians have done over the last 8 months to hide from their people the fact that Russian soldiers have been killed in Ukraine, it is really extraordinary.

And I would actually argue it is disgraceful. Reports of Russian soldiers being buried at night, reports of Russian casualties hidden. I head a story from a friend of my wife in Moscow who said somebody lost their leg fighting in Donetsk in August, and he has been told if you disclose that publicly, you will lose your pension forever.

So I think there really is a real concern in Moscow that casualties could have an impact. And I am not sure that Mr. Putin cares per se about Russian soldiers and casualties, but I think he does care a lot about the impact of that on the Russian public's attitude and their attitudes towards him. And this is against the background of 4 or 5 months of polls that show that while the Russian people may support trying to pull Ukraine back toward Russia, majorities do not want to see the Russian Army fighting in Ukraine.

So I think there is—I would make the argument that there is a good chance that, in fact, this could succeed in altering that cost benefit calculation to the point where the Russians would say military escalation makes no more sense because we are going have casualties. It will require overt involvement by the Russian Army, and, therefore, we want to pursue a peaceful settlement.

We do in our report—nobody who wrote the report—we are not recommending American combat troops. We even said that the equipment that would be provided has to be operated by the Ukrainians so you would not have American technicians there. I would say we are not in a position to provide advanced offensive arms. We are going to have some limit, and I would argue that you need to make that limit clear to the Ukrainians privately so that they know what to expect. But we can make a firebreak that prevents us from getting caught into an endless spiral of escalation with the Russians that, I would argue, then keeps us safely on the side of not going into a direct United States-Russian military confrontation.

Senator MURPHY. Let me just ask my second question quickly, Damon. You talk about the fact that some European allies would support us, some would not. Putin has a lot of goals here, but one of them is to break Europe. And so, this would be convenient for him to have half of Europe supporting defensive weapons, half not. What is the potential consequences of Europe not being together on this? As many have said, the ultimate win here is that the Russian economy suffers under the tremendous weight of the sanctions such that it changes his position. But are we not going to risk losing countries like the Czech Republic, or the Hungarians, or the Greeks if we start to split over issues of military arming, or can we hold folks together on everything else besides the question of defensive weapons?

Mr. WILSON. I think many of our allies expect the United States to actually lead here. And it would not be unusual if you look at controversial decisions in the alliance where the United States is out front, has key allies stand with it and some others stand behind it. The United States is rarely in the middle of the pack there. This is risky. It is not a no-brainer as you say. I do not think it is the kind of thing that would lead to an overt split within the alliance.

We saw even over something as sensitive as Iraq, which was a very divisive issue within the alliance, we still were able to craft an agreement of a NATO training mission in Iraq after the fact and find something that brought the allies together. And I think that would be an important part of this element to this narrative that not only does the United States move forward with some other allies in concert bilaterally, but there is actually a NATO component in which all the allies are playing a role in supporting Ukraine, not with arming, but with a defense reform and a defense package.

Your original point I think, however, is right. We are obsessed with the issue as the issue of the day. Putin, I think, is looking to win right now financially. I think the time sensitive part is the collapse of the economy. I think that is a real danger right now even as we debate weapons. And second, the weapons are effective if we have a strategy, part of a broader strategy, where Putin looks up and he realizes that we—I mean, we are far stronger across the board.

You mentioned Serbia, and American strategy that is moving on NATO and Montenegro, and actually working to deepen the partnership with Serbia to show that we actually pushed back in asymmetric ways as well I think helps to fill out a more comprehensive strategy, weapons being an essential element of that, but not the only element.

Senator JOHNSON. Mr. Kasparov.

Mr. KASPAROV. Senator Murphy mentioned Czechoslovakia, Hungary, Poland, certain interventions in Eastern Europe. But I do not think that we can compare the situation with Ukraine because the Soviet Union, as much as I hate this kind of action, operated within a sphere of influence agreed to in Yalta in 1945, so the world was divided. Today it is totally different because we can look at the collapse of the Soviet Union or the collapse of Yugoslavia, all new states. Even Yugoslavia has 7 new states, including Kosovo. They were all formed within the territory of administrative borders created within the empire. So all of them, whether they are right or wrong, you know, there was an agreement.

And if you look at Ukraine, every Russian President, every Russian Parliament signed or ratified one or another form of treaty or agreement with Ukraine, and Russia never, ever expressed any concerns about Ukrainian territorial integrity, never raised an issue. Even Saddam Hussein raised an issue on Kuwait. Hitler talked about Sudetenland or Danzig. Russia never raised this issue, so that is why it is absolutely unique. And this attack is unprecedented because it violated not only agreements, but also the understanding of how the world would be split after the end of the cold war.

Senator MURPHY. I do not disagree. I think that is a very good point.

Thank you, Mr. Chairman.

Mr. SAAKASHVILI. Senator?

Senator MURPHY. Sure.

Mr. SAAKASHVILI. Senator, first of all, I need to thank you for your intervention on Ukraine. I was there together with group of European parliamentarians just before you came. And I remember—and then we were proclaimed persona non grata, and then your visit, by the way, together with the other U.S. colleagues, really changed the equation that came at right moment because they were really losing steam, you know. They had this little bit of frustration were being abandoned. And you being there, it really changed the whole idea of what the Ukrainian revolution was about, and it made it very much value-oriented.

Now, there is another story there which is not only just weapons story in Ukraine, bit about United States involvement. It is a good story. And it also has to do something with my country because what happened in Ukraine that Georgia—that some members of my government became members of Ukrainian Government. That is also very unique experience. Our Minister of Interior has become their first Deputy Minister of Interior of Ukraine, and she is running the reform of Ukraine with the United States, with USAID.

They fired the entire Kiev traffic police, and they go city by city. And this is American money. This lady is Georgian, and they are together creating new Ukrainian police that will show how to work and operate without bribes. That had never happened before in that part of the world, or at least in Ukraine.

Then there is another story. We have our Deputy Minister of Justice from Georgia there who is working also with your programs and also, by the way, with U.S. Congress funded NGOs that are doing tremendous job in the regulation, you know. Their bureaucracies like something that unimaginable in terms of, you know, discretion of bureaucrats and, you know, how they do this corruption thing. This is, again, the Americans doing that together with that.

We have Minister of Health who just had long conference together with American donors and U.S. Ambassadors involved there on the spot. And they are doing now absolute new transparent procedures, how to do these tenders and things which never also happened in Ukraine. It was a major source of corruption traditionally. We have deputy attorney general for Ukraine, which is Georgian, foreign deputy attorney general of Ukraine. And now we are bringing—we invited U.S. experts to sit down together with them because they are working high profile criminal cases. And, again, there is the anticorruption bureau will be created where also there be activity for U.S. expert participation.

So it is not only about weapons. I think long term Ukraine's survival and Ukraine's strategy should be based on the idea that they have something else to offer besides military things. But this should all be just be packed up with something else as well. Thank you.

Dr. BLANK. I would like just to make two points very quickly. The discussion about weapons is insufficient in the sense that weapons, to realize their maximum benefit for Ukraine, have to be sent urgently, but as part of a broader strategy to rebuild the Ukrainian Government and economy, which is also an urgent issue, and as an information strategy. I mentioned in my paper no one is talking about the number of casualties the Russians are taking, which are huge. We are doing nothing informationally to counter the wave of propaganda.

Furthermore, to the extent that the United States leads the Atlantic alliance, not only will NATO members follow, or at least accept what we are doing, we will have also changed the balance of fear because right now the Russians are not afraid of anything that Europe might do. As President Saakashvili has pointed out, when the Russians understand that if they go further they encounter United States directly, they stop. They even on occasion retreat.

And finally, we have done this before. Let me remind you about Afghanistan where we gave very sophisticated weapons to people directly in the line of Soviet aggression, and it worked. This is not the Soviet Union. This is an army that cannot stand the protracted war or take that kind of risk, and, therefore, providing weapons will, I think, help stabilize and perhaps even turn the situation around if it is backed up by a coherent strategy.

Senator JOHNSON. Senator Kaine. Thanks for your patience.

Senator KAINE. Absolutely. It has all been educational, and thank you, Mr. Chairman, and thanks to all the witnesses.

Three topics. First on the sanctions and economic effect on Russia right now, it sounds as if one of the takeaways from today should be work that we need to do with Europe to make sure the annual re-up of the sanctions, you know, the continuity has got to be our message, our very strong message to the Europeans. And I gather that everybody is on board with that. We need to do more on our side. The President did more today, and there is more that Congress can do.

But I am particularly interested in the low cost of oil as a perennial problem for the Russian economy. And it is not just a problem for the Russian economy. It is also a problem for the Iranian economy, which is a separate topic. That is a very important issue for us now.

What are other things we can do in the energy space, whether it is sanctions or whether it is assisting European nations with energy technologies? We have had a fairly contentious debate on this committee about things like LNG exports, even to send the signal that that would be something we would contemplate into the region to help nations break their need to rely too much on energy. Talk a little bit about low energy costs and what we ought to be doing to continue to pressure the Russian economy using that as a strategy, please, Dr. Blank.

Dr. BLANK. There are a number of things we can be doing. We can increase the export of oil and of LNG, which would require, of course, building infrastructure here, as well as amending legislation. But oil can be already sent. It was reported last year that we could send 40 million barrels a day for 6 months without undermining the statute or without reversing the meaning of the statute, guaranteeing the strategic petroleum reserve. We could probably still do that. We can further encourage much more strongly the building of the southern corridor of gas across the Caspian Sea and provide strong guarantees to countries like Azerbaijan, Turkmenistan, and so on, that want to make that happen.

And third, to promote not only the building of interconnectors within Europe so that new terminals that are being built in Northern Europe and the Baltic can then move gas to the south, but also if we pass the TTIP, that makes every European signatory of the treaty eligible to receive gas exports from the United States on an expedited basis without going through the very convoluted bureaucratic procedure. Once that law is in place, they can then get gas from the United States, and we can supplant a fair amount of the Russian gas exports, which is what Russia uses for political purposes.

The problem is not Russia exports gas and oil to Europe. The problem is that they can do so and use that for political purposes. If it becomes a straight commercial transaction, well and good. But to the extent that they have politicized this, we need to take that weapon away from them.

Senator KAINE. Other thoughts on the energy space?

Ambassador PIFER. Yes. I would just, Senator, just add on the LNG. My understanding is that the United States is now building to the point where by about 2020 we could export between $100 and $120 billion cubic meters of gas per year, which would be, I think, a sizable increase in gas stocks. Right now, my understanding is in most of Europe now, they actually have significant capacity to import LNG. They have, in fact, remained reliant on the Russians because the Russian gas in the pipeline is cheaper.

Senator KAINE. Right.

Ambassador PIFER. But what we want to make sure is that Europe has the capacity that if the Russians were ever to turn the gas off, which I do not think is likely, and I will get back to that in a moment. But that they, in fact, could continue receiving LNG, and it gets to Dr. Blank's points about building interconnectors, which are now pretty good in most of Europe, but there are still areas—Romania, Bulgaria, Greece—that are still vulnerable until they get some more interconnectors that would allow gas to move from the West to the East.

I think, though, at the end of the day, it is hard for me to see the Russians, Gazprom, ever turning that gas off. It is almost—it is a mutual deterrent relationship in that Europe needs the gas, so they want the cheaper Russian gas because it is cheaper than LNG. But if Gazprom turns that gas off, it is a huge hole in the Russian budget because they use that large amount of money that they make by exporting the gas to Europe.

I saw figures, and these are maybe about 4 years out of date, where about 25 percent of Gazprom exports went to Europe, but that accounted for about 70 percent of Gazprom revenues. So Gazprom has a big incentive not to do this, but it still makes sense for Europe to have a plan B in case the Russians ever reach that point where they micht cut off the gas flow.

Senator KAINE. Mr. Kasparov, I wanted to ask you a question. You want to comment on that before I ask you the question?

Mr. KASPAROV. Yes. It was said here numerous times about the importance of keeping sanctions or even, you know, increasing the sanctions. And, of course, that problem is in Europe. But sanctions, apart from economic effect, they have psychological effect, and so far Putin has succeeded in convincing not only the Russian republic, but the Russian elite, that these sanctions will not stand. So somehow, you know—and he has enough friends, you know. Let us not forget, Czech Republic, President Zeman, has been financed by Lukoil openly. Open. Now, it is probably Russian subsidies. Greeks, you know.

You can look around Europe and you will find so many traces of Putin's actions, you know, and lobbying efforts that are unfortunately quite successful. But it is very important, you know, that Putin could point out multinational corporations that are still operating, and in that sense, you know, a signal of confidence. Just 2 days ago, Exxon-Mobil has announced about expansion of its operations in Russia. I mean, that is a fundamental, you know, argument for Putin—okay, Obama, Presidents, you know, Prime Ministers, the business is still here.

And as long as we have this presence in Russia, as long as we have business as usual, it will be very difficult to win the psychological war because expectations could actually destroy the Russian economy even sooner than economic——

Senator KAINE. I agree with you. I think there is a psychological impact. And even if you knew LNG would not get there for 2 years, you start to do things that sends a message, and similarly with energy sanctions. I am a big supporter of sanctions in the energy space. That is the lever that is being used. That is where we ought to sanction.

Mr. Kasparov, I wanted to switch to another topic, which is, you know, we tend to look at these things through the eyes of political people. From your experience, what will it take? What are the kinds of conditions that will cause Vladimir Putin to lose political support within his electorate, within Russian citizens, because there is outside pressure, but the most effective pressure is often the inside pressure when the population starts to pull their support from you.

You talked about the propaganda regime, et cetera, makes it difficult for the message to get through. But from your experience, what will cause a decrease in the domestic political support for Vladimir Putin?

Mr. KASPAROV. Unfortunately, I do not see sort of a positive outcome in the near future. Vladimir Putin is not going to lose his powers through the normal election process, so he is there. He is a dictator, and he made it very clear that he would not leave the office. The good thing is that, you know, a country so hyper-centralized as Russia does not have much political activities outside of the capital. So basically even if he enjoys this 80 percent plus support, which I do not believe, across the country, what matters is Moscow, and we know that numbers in Moscow are very different.

Even St. Petersburg, today has turned into some form of political province. Whatever happens in Moscow could determine the future of Russia. And we have a pretty sizable middle class in Russia that is used to a relatively comfortable life. They travel abroad, and I do not think this middle class will accept sort of long-term decline of the standards that have been established.

For quite a while—for many years actually—this middle class has been relatively silent. So we saw some of the protests in the 2011, 2012. People did not like what has happened with the elections, but, again, it was not powerful enough. The coalition was not there because the ruling elite believed that that it was better to stay with Putin than to join the protests.

What will change everything is that if people in the ruling elite, some in the inner circle, and, of course, the Russian middle class.

They all recognize that Russia will have no future with Vladimir Putin. Stop appealing to Putin. He is irrelevant because he burned all the bridges. You have to look for people who can end his rule with minimum bloodshed. And I think it is—as long as Putin stays in office, we will see more political assassinations, more attacks on neighboring countries because that is the only algorithm where he can survive. I think that America has many ways of demonstrating it, and talking about European Union is exactly the opposite, you know.

Putin gained so much influence in Europe because America walked away, so only American reappearance there will send a signal because everybody wants to see leadership. And I know Baltic States well. Forget Germany. I mean, remember in 2003, it was rumored that someone in the Bush administration, summarized the policy at the time as, ''Punish France, Ignore Germany, and Forgive Russia.'' So basically ignore Germany, because Angela Merkel is the head of the coalition government, and her Foreign Minister belongs to Gerhard Schroeder's party. So expecting from this fragile coalition government to lead Europe is wrong.

So that is why America's presence is paramount. Without it, nothing will happen. And it will send signal not only to Ukraine, not only to Poles, but also to Russian people that, you know, America is back to business.

Senator KAINE. Okay, Mr. Chairman, if others wanted to weigh in on that question. I do not have any other questions, but I would love to hear their responses.

Senator JOHNSON. Mr. Blank.

Dr. BLANK. Yes, in response to your last question, undermining Putin's domestic base of support is a long-term operation. But it requires the systematic application of a strategy to tell the truth, to use the information capabilities that we have for maximum strategic effect, and broadcast to the Russian people just how bad the situation is inside Russia and where Putin is leading them. And that will in time do so.

Furthermore, as Mr. Kasparov said, it is essential for the United States not only to lead in Europe, but to stop showing fear and disengagement. And this will also have an encouraging effect upon Europe as well. Third, we have to remember, if we look at Russian history, that it is always the case that when the Russian Government enters into a protracted war which it cannot win, that creates domestic unrest at home. Therefore, sending the weapons and making sure that the Ukrainian economy and government survive is not only desirable as an urgent remedy right now to impose costs on the war, but it transforms not only the balance of fear in Europe and Ukraine, it transforms the strategic calculations inside Russia because then you create the pressures that have historically worked to undermine this kind of government.

Senator JOHNSON. Ambassador Pifer.

Ambassador PIFER. Thank you, sir. I would like to just make two points, one on sanctions. I would go back to the logic of the sanctions and go back to something that was being said about Russia and Vladimir Putin maybe in 2003, 2004 where Russians talked about President Putin having an implicit social compact with the Russian people, in which he says you are not going to have any political say, but in return, you will have economic security, rising living standards. You are going to see the economy do well. Sanctions make it more difficult for Mr. Putin to deliver on his part of that bargain, and that, I think, may have an impact on how the Russian people look at him.

The second point just briefly, I would give a little bit more charitable analysis of Germany. I think actually Chancellor Merkel has been remarkably successful in pulling together the European Union, 28 diverse states with very different views. And for her, at least what I hear from German diplomats, at core, it is a principle. She really takes to heart the idea that borders are inviolable, and that countries should not use force to change those borders.

So with her taking that role, I think at some political risk because this is not easy either internally or also dealing with the Russians. But she has played a very good role, and it makes a lot of sense for the United States to be working very closely with her in that role to sustain the sort of unity that we have built with Europe over the last year.

Senator KAINE. Mr. President.

Mr. SAAKASHVILI. Yes. With regards to Russia, I mean, it is very clear that, first of all, the idea of this hearing obviously is what will happen next. And I can tell you, I met with Putin dozens of times. He always told me three things consistently, that he was menacing us with invasion, he will always mention that Ukraine is not a real country, it is just a territory, and, third, he always said that Baltic countries are not defendable. He always says beforehand what he wants. People have heard it.

And it is very clear that what—if he gets away with Ukraine, then Baltic countries, which do not have even strategic depth or manpower of Ukrainians, they just rely on United States Article 5 guarantees, which is important stuff. But still, I mean, there are many vulnerabilities that they have, even more than the Ukrainians ever had. That is very clear that he will continue on because that is the only way how he sees he can maintain power inside Russia.

Now, when we talk about his 80 percent rating, we should realize that this is a fear rating. This is not real in population. People tend to measure it with measurements of democracies, and that does not work this way in these kind of systems. You know, I think North Korean leader has even higher ratings. It does not mean that, you know.

So what it means is that basically people have been saying, well, Russians cannot stand just any sanctions, you know, that is the history of Russia. I think this is not true simply because Russia has never had such a strong middle class. This is combination first of the United States assistance, bailing out the Russian economy in the 1990s, which really was the decisive factor, and then, of course, the oil price and redistributing it inside Russia.

This middle class has always lived with expanded living standards. They are not used to living with a decline in living standards. Nobody has seen them. So it makes Putin panic. It makes Putin make mistakes and to become more aggressive. And I think shale gas—generally U.S. shale gas—is the single most important factor in what has brought him into this panic mode.

What United States did with its legal system, which does not happen in Europe, is that in Europe you can, you know, manipulate some environmental groups and others, block local shale production because whatever is underground basically belongs to the state. Here it belongs to the person who owns the land. And that makes the U.S. system so much more open to this kind of entrepreneurial enterprise. So that really changed the whole logic of the event. Suddenly, good guys have energy and bad guys have lower money for their energy. So from that standpoint, it is absolutely deciding factor.

I think that it is not—it is a matter of not many years that a thing has emerged, there is a physical fatigue. Every leader, even the most autocratic one, has his time span. I think Chinese have been smarter with that. They have been changing the faces of their leaders, and they have a more flexible system here. This is a one-man show. You know, everything—there is no other political actor. He played around a little bit with other ideas. Gone. Now, it is him. All credit is taken by him. Every blame goes to him. And that is a very dangerous system for no matter which politician. From that standpoint, I am very optimistic.

The Russian people are well-read people, they are well-traveled people. They certainly want to be respected internationally, although until now they had it both ways. They were getting away with playing around in the neighborhood. They were being nasty. And at the time, they still kept some kind of resemblance of respect. Now, those two are not compatible, and people will understand it.

And, again, going back, I fully agree with Steven. The Afghan syndrome is very important. When I was in the Soviet Union, I remember what the combination of low oil prices and MANPADS did. Until low prices, it would not have worked, but now you have the lower prices suddenly, so budgetary income went down, and then MANPADS reversed the logic on the ground. That is exactly what we have now. We have lower oil and gas prices, and we just need some Javelins, or whatever the Ukrainians will be requesting, to change the cost of that equation. After all, cost equation matters, maybe even not for Putin, but for the Russians or the Russian public, whatever elite is left there, security apparatus, it will certainly make lots of difference, and that is my main hope. Thank you.

Senator KAINE. Thank you, Mr. Chairman.

Senator JOHNSON. Thank you, Senator Kaine. I would like to go back to the story. I would like somebody to talk to the courage of the Ukrainian people. Senator Murphy talked about being in the Maidan. I was heartened, I was encouraged by my colleagues here in the Senate and the House unanimously passing the Ukraine Freedom Support Act, which did authorize lethal defense weaponry for the courageous people of Ukraine. The reason I think we did that is because so many of us went over there. I was with Senator Murphy with a bipartisan delegation, about eight U.S. Senators, and we walked the Maidan. We heard the story of the sniper attack.

I would like to hear the story of the rebellion, the pushback from the Ukrainian military that had been hollowed out purposefully, but also the courage of the Ukrainian people defending themselves, turning the tide, and then having that tide turned back against them because of Russian involvement, the Russia's invasion with 14,000 to 20,000 troops and heavy weapons. I want to enter those pictures into the record.

[The photographs referred to by Senator Johnson are located at the end of this hearing transcript, beginning on page 59.]

Senator JOHNSON. I want somebody to speak to that—somebody to answer the question—to answer the plea of President Poroshenko when he came before a joint session of this Congress and said that blankets and night vision goggles are important, he said, but one cannot win a war with blankets.

Can somebody here just talk about what has happened in the military campaign against the rebels, how the tide had turned, how it had been turned back again, and then how desperate the situation is? One of the reasons I held this hearing this week, kind of rushed it, is because we heard last week that there was potentially an offensive being planned within the next few weeks. We heard that earlier, potentially a spring offensive.

Can somebody just talk about the history of this military conflict, this rebellion, what will likely happen and how desperate the situation is?

Dr. BLANK. Well, I can try to answer as much as possible that question. The Russians have been behind the attempt to squelch the revolution from the beginning, even when it was just simply a demonstration on the Maidan. We know that Russian advisors were telling Yanukovych's government to repress them and use force if necessary. We also have good reason to believe—I was told this by Ukrainian politicians in October 2013 when the issue was signing the association agreement with the European Union, which led to the revolution, that Putin threatened Ukrainian with invasion then if they signed. And there were analysts in this town, myself among them, who warned at that point that Putin was doing that. We were disregarded.

The fact of the matter is that the Ukrainian people have sacrificed what the Declaration of Independence calls their lives, their fortunes, and their sacred honor—their sacred honor, to live freely and independently, and to make it clear that they wanted a better life, which meant that an association with Europe and European forms of government.

This is intolerable to Moscow for the reasons we talked about today. Empire is the only recourse Moscow has to save it kleptocratic autocracy. It has become a criminalized regime, a state that exports terror, as well as uses it at home, and there is no denying that. He has done it in Georgia, he has done it at home, and he is doing it in Ukrainian.

The operation to seize Crimea was started before February 21. We know this. For example, the medals that the Russian President gave out to his troops dates the operation from February 20, the day before the EU agreement with Yanukovych. Yanukovych then fled that night anyway, but the Russians were already active. And the only reason they did not go faster is because the troops there were supposed to lead that operation in Crimea, were guarding the Olympics in Sochi, which ended only February 23.

This is a cold-blooded premeditated aggression. It caught the Ukrainian Government and Army by complete surprise, and as a result they lost Crimea. Then they started to use the organizational tools they had previously set up in Donetsk and Luhansk Cabanas and provinces to agitate there. They took advantage of some ill-considered decisions by the new government on language policy and created a pretext for an invasion in March into April.

That went forward, but Putin thought he could get away with doing that simply by giving the arms and some direction to locally organized forces. That proved to be impossible. As a matter of fact, they shot down MH317 as we know, and they were in danger of losing in August when Putin then had to commit Russian regular forces.

Since then, Putin has had to escalate his commitment and basically take over the entire military operation. Now, the entire military operation from start to finish was predicated on creating on what this new Russia, Novorossiya, a term that goes back to Catherine the Great 250 years ago. In fact, it is an attempt to destroy Ukraine, create a land bridge from Russia all the way across Southern Ukraine and Crimea to Transnistria, and project Russian power not only through Ukraine, but into the Balkans and Black Sea and beyond. Moscow has even sought military and naval bases in Greece, Montenegro, and Serbia.

It is, I believe, using this truce to replenish its forces. The amount of ammunition that the Russians have expended because their tactics are essentially basically artillery pounding, has been enormous. And they are surprised, according to my sources, at how much they had to use in August and now again in January to achieve their objectives. Therefore, they have to call a halt, they signed onto Minsk, and are trying to get a truce so they can replenish. But I have no doubt that come springtime they will make a move on, if not earlier, on Mariupol and the entire Black Sea coast of Ukraine, and perhaps all the way through Odessa as well.

So, therefore, that is a kind of survey of the entire military operation from start to finish. But the start was not February 2014. The start is 2005 when the first attempt by Moscow to seize Ukraine failed in 2004.

Senator JOHNSON. Anybody else just want to speak to the courage of the Ukrainian people and why they need to be supported?

Mr. SAAKASHVILI. Well, I want to speak about a pilot, Nadia Savchenko, who was kidnapped and is being held. She is a military pilot, was active participant of the Maidan protests. And she was kidnapped from the Ukrainian territory, brought to Russia. She is now held in Moscow. And she is in grave medical condition because she has been going through a hunger strike. And, you know, there are many Ukrainians like that that sacrifice their lives.

The remarkable story of Ukraine is not just heroism on the battlefield, which was very obvious. You know, these are the troops that were technological, that for 10 years or so they were just plundering everything, giving up everything for legal means, but also illegal means. There was lots of corruption while Russia was building up things. So that reality came into being totally. They were taken by surprise, unprepared, untrained, and still, against all the odds, were holding out for a long time against Russian forces and are continuing to do so.

Now, the important thing to understand there is another aspect to this fight. Most of these efforts of the Ukrainian army have been done also by volunteers, supplying the troops, medical supplies, even military supplies and the bulletproof vests, you know, there have been thousands and tens of thousands. And in the case of money, millions of Ukrainians contributed. It is not just war of Putin versus Poroshenko or, you know, it is against the Ukrainian Government. It is Putin's war against the multiethnic Ukrainian nation.

The other thing people do not really know here is that most of the troops fighting and protecting Ukraine are Russian speakers, and basically big part of them are ethnic Russians. This is not an ethnic issue. This is not, you know—this is not a regional issue. This is not, as I said, government-to-government issue. This is the multiethnic, multicultural nation of Ukraine trying to defend its freedom, its values, and its ideals. And the whole society's part of it, because as I said, the government was almost bankrupt, and you had people volunteering and basically supplying most of the things they are getting there.

And I do not know any other country in the world where this number of volunteers, so large a part for the population has been engaged in what is an all-around national campaign for the nation's survival. And that is something to be considered for all of us because, you know, again, as I said, I told you about Georgia volunteers fighting there. Basically most of them, you know, they are not there for money. They are not paid anything, but whatever they are supplied with, these are given by ordinary Ukrainians. This is not the government that gives them that.

Senator JOHNSON. I will let everybody else summarize. I want to be respectful of Senator Shaheen. She has a question, and then I will let everybody wrap up and give my final thoughts.

Senator SHAHEEN. Thank you very much, Mr. Chairman. I wanted to go back to the economic concerns because one of you I think—I am not sure who—suggested that support for weapons may be moot if the economy fails in Ukraine before that happens. And I know that the IMF has pledged funding as has the EU and the United States, of course.

But to what extent can the Ukrainian economy, and President Poroshenko, and the government survive the reforms that are being asked of it, and keep the economy afloat, and continue this military conflict at the same time? And what more can the United States do to help with that? Damon, do you want to start?

Mr. WILSON. Senator, I think that is exactly one of my key concerns right now is that there may be a rationale for the military fighting to die down. Putin does not need to own two slices of Donetsk and Luhansk. He needs all of Ukraine. And I think part of the strategy that I am most concerned about right now is which economy collapses first, and can he raise Ukraine—can he push Ukraine's off the cliff first.

This is why I have been, on the one hand, alarmed at how long and difficult it has been to get a significant international package together that includes the U.S.'s catalytic, but the IMF and the EU will add more. And at the same time, we are asking Ukrainians to do some quite difficult reforms. I think this is the moment.

President Poroshenko and Prime Minister Yatsenyuk, they understand that they have had predecessors that had an opportunity to build a new Ukraine, and they failed at the time of independence, at the time of the Orange Revolution. They do not have many other shots at it. And so, despite the difficulty, I think being able to communicate to the Ukrainian people that in this time of existential crisis is when they need to take some pretty dramatic steps. And we just saw the Rada pass very significant legislation which will begin to raise overall energy prices and begin to address some structural economic issues.

But the gap there I think is a much more robust and much more decisive intervention on the part of the international community providing that economic assistance and providing that comfort because this is the race that I think—Putin can let it sit for a while, allow his little project Sparta to build up its weapons, and try to go for all of the Ukraine by driving down the economy, after all, trying to drive the collapse of this government.

Senator SHAHEEN. Anyone else want to comment on that? Ambassador Pifer and then Dr. Blank.

Ambassador PIFER. Yes, Senator. No, I think this is why we need to talk about a multipronged strategy. I mean, it is has got to be not just providing arms. It has also got to be maintaining sanctions. It has also got to be doing the economic finance, which I think will be costly. The IMF program, as I understand it, is for $17.5 billion over 4 years. I have heard some economists suggest that in 2015 and 2016, above and beyond that Ukraine could need an additional $20 to $22 billion.

If we provide all the weapons in the world, and they hold the Russians off, and they stabilize line of contact, and the economy collapses, the West has lost its policy goal. Likewise, if we make the economy work, if we get them through the reforms, but then they have the military collapse, that is a loss. We have got to be doing both these pieces at the same time. And I think we have to face up to it. It will require probably an injection of serious resources both by Europe and the United States.

Senator SHAHEEN. Thank you.

Dr. Blank.

Dr. BLANK. I would add to that, that while everything my colleagues have said I agree with, that what is critical here as well I think is the psychological dimension. We are asking Ukrainians to do something of an extraordinarily difficult nature, and they have not the sense that we stand behind them. On the other hand, if they were aware and understood that they had the full support of the United States and of Europe, and that they were not alone, that would provide an enormous psychological strength and reinforce other European states' ability and willingness to help them. And it would undermine a great deal of Russia's strategy.

Therefore, all these factors come together—the provision of weapons and training, the economic and political assistance, and the overwhelming psychological assurance that you are not alone.

Senator SHAHEEN. I certainly agree with that. We have sent mixed signals, and I would hope that Ukraine would know that we are behind them 100 percent. I do hope that this Congress can pass the reforms to the IMF, too, because that would allow us additional assistance as we are looking where can we provide economic assistance to Ukraine.

President Saakashvili.

Mr. SAAKASHVILI. Well, I have just to add that besides $17 billion, overall pledge is $40 billion for the reform package. It is very important United States—we are trying to now jumpstart the reforms, but it is very important also this committee and generally overall the U.S. Congress pays greater attention. We need more CODELs coming, and specifically not only with a focus on military issue, which is urgent issue because it has become tantamount to the symbol of whether Ukraine is abandoned or not, but it is beyond that. What is really needed is real crackdown on corruption, real economic changes, really for ordinary Ukrainians to see the difference.

And from that standpoint, from our own experience in Georgia, the United States standing by the idea of reform, we are steering in right direction, you know, giving incentives, giving praise when necessary and sometimes offering friendly criticism when it is also necessary. It is absolutely key for reforms inside Ukraine to know what has been there for decades, invested interests, you know, of plundering and basically robbing that is potentially a very rich nation with very smart people and very talented people.

And I think this is the best Parliament they ever had right now. It is more clean of any previous legislatures, so it is very easy to work through these parliamentarians. Many of them are quite inexperienced, so they need to be introduced also to the U.S. system. You need to bring them here as well. You need to get know them—get to know them, you know.

And I think there is—that reminds of what—we were like this in mid-1990s. And I remember our first—I was parliamentarian back in 1996, fresh from GW law school here. And I remember coming back every time, every 3, 4, 5, 6 months together with a bunch of younger parliamentarians, not just to talk to you or ask for help, but to learn, to get educated, you know, and exchange ideas. That was absolutely the single strongest factor behind Georgian democracy, somehow getting stronger and also communication with people. And I think Ukrainians see this more than ever. And I think you are all here deciding—I think this hearing also has a key role to play for that.

Senator SHAHEEN. Well, thank you all very much for your compelling testimony and for your continued focus on Ukraine. And thank you, Mr. Chairman, for this hearing.

Senator JOHNSON. Thank you, and I want to thank all of my colleagues for attending. I will just give everybody a chance to quickly wrap up. We will go in reverse order. We will start with Ambassador Pifer. If there is something that you have not been able to get out, please say it.

Ambassador PIFER. Thank you, Senator. I guess I would come back to one point about how far the Russians want to go. And although I do not exclude that the Russians might try to go all the way to Crimea to create the land bridge, I worry a little bit less about that than I think Dr. Blank does. It has been interesting that in the last 5 or 6 months, I do not think Vladimir Putin has mentioned the term ''Novorossiya'' once. And what I hope that means is he understands that the further West the Russians go, the more they are going to encounter a hostile population and the possibility of partisan warfare. Having said that, I still think the Russians have a lot of possibilities just fighting along the current line without a major offensive to distract and destabilize the government in Kiev, and that may be their cheaper option.

My final point would be whether we are concerned more about the big option of going to Crimea or just having more of a not so frozen conflict along the line of conflict. Providing weapons in the context of sanctions and economic assistance to Ukraine is a way to challenge or to change that calculation in Moscow, and hopefully bring the Russians to conclude that fighting no longer is worthwhile, and that they have to find a way to finally take that diplomatic off ramp.

Senator JOHNSON. Thank you, Mr. Ambassador. Mr. Wilson, one final thought?

Mr. WILSON. Senator, I wanted to go back to your last statement because I think it was one of the most important things here about the Ukrainian people. I think that is one of the most factors that outside actors actually under appreciate. Ukraine is the victim of the tyranny of low expectations. President Putin could not imagine that the Ukrainian people could rise up and determine their future. They were skeptical of the fact that the Ukrainians would even have a common national identity. And the irony of his invasion of Ukraine has more to consolidate and strengthen that sense of identity and purpose than any single thing. If we play this right, this is actually a 500-year defeat for Russia to have actually lost a country like Ukraine, which is a natural partner, a natural neighbor, and decisively having turned that country to the West.

And yet the West also has a tyranny of low expectations toward Ukraine. If you talk to our Treasury officials, IMF officials, they are skeptical that Ukraine is a good investment. We have seen this fail before. If you talk to realists, they think, well, we can just cut a deal over the Ukrainian people's heads, that this country will never go to NATO. I do not think that works any more. That is not—President Poroshenko himself has now real constraints. I was there when protestors were outside his office because he was willing to agree to a cease-fire. The Ukrainian people now have a say in the future of what is going to happen, and I think outsiders underestimate that factor that the Maidan was genuine, and it is what drove this from the beginning.

So I would just conclude with, we should remember how all of this started, that Ukrainians were actually willing to die for this concept of Europe, for a Europe which is at best skeptical about even wanting Ukraine as part of the European Union. And so, that leads me back to where we fit into this.

The entire chapter of integration in Europe has been driven by U.S. leadership, it is European integration, driven by the United States, being a great European power, providing the framework and helping that happen. If we stand back and think of ourselves as an observer as this unfolds, as an observer of what Europe and Ukraine will do together, I think this will fail. But if we see ourselves as a driver of helping to support the European aspirations of Ukraine, I think we can get this right.

Senator JOHNSON. Thank you. President Obama said we are the indispensable Nation. In addition to looking to Europe, the other aspiration really was a corruption free Ukraine. It is a combination of both of those elements that created that courage.

Dr. Blank.

Dr. BLANK. Thank you, Senator. I just want to leave the committee with the thought that on March 12, 1947, President Truman stood in the Capitol and said that it was the policy of the United States to support free peoples. And at that time, he was responding to a Soviet challenge in the Black Sea, Greece and Turkey, in particular.

That mission has not changed, and as Damon has said, if we are to see a Europe that is whole and free, we must help lead the process. We cannot be disengaged or lead from behind because then we just open up Europe to the ancient horrors that we now see taking over, of autocratic warlike criminal governments seizing territories at their whim.

The people of Ukraine have shed their own blood in order get their freedom. As I mentioned, they have pledged their sacred honor, their fortunes, and their lives, and we can do no less. Thank you.

Senator JOHNSON. Thank you, Doctor.

Mr. Kasparov.

Mr. KASPAROV. Yes. I think we should pay attention to Putin's propaganda machine, and it is a fact that we could see and hear in Europe and in the United States. Many people believe, as President Saakashvili mentioned, that it is an ethnic conflict. There were over 23 years of existence of independent Ukraine, maybe with the exception of Crimea when it was a rogue political group that made 4 percent of the elections.

Ukraine did not have any political movement for secession unlike Catalonia or Scotland. So those are examples that the Russian Government wants to bring in, or Kosovo. There was always a movement, even Ireland you had, you know, terrorist groups, but also the political wing. So there were political movements demanding independence. We never heard of the existence of such groups in Ukraine. So that is why when I read in the Minsk agreement about the political settlement, I still do not understand who is going to settle on the opposite side, the gangs supported by Putin because political groups in Eastern Ukraine never created a core entity that specifically asked for independence.

And, of course, it is important to mention that most of the people fighting in East Ukraine, they are Russians on both sides, ethnic Russians. And as Ambassador Pifer mentioned, the term, Novorossiya, has disappeared completely because Putin realized that his grandiose plan of bringing eight Ukrainian regions all the way down from Luhansk from Odessa to have the corridor to both Crimea and Moldova failed because ethnic Russians did not want to embrace Russian troops. Moreover, he could experience resistance even in Donetsk and Luhansk, so not mentioning, you know, further south and west to Dnipropetrovsk or Harikov.

So it is a war that has an aggressor who is trying to use this ethnic card, but we have to reveal the true nature of the conflict. A Ukrainian nation has been formed, and this is a nation that wants to be in Europe, and it is a multi-ethnic community. Russian has been widely spoken there. If I understand correctly, more channels in Ukraine are using Russian than Ukraine or major TV talk shows in Ukraine that are run by journalists who have Russian as their first language. So this Putin propaganda machine should be confronted with a strong message that we are not going to buy these arguments, which unfortunately are still being bought by Europeans.

And summarizing this. We talked about, you know, the sanctions and about actions of Western governments vis-a-vis the commercial or economic interests of Putin's Russia. But let us not forget about the damage made by Russian propaganda called Russian Roulette. It spreads lies to millions and millions of homes around the world, and it is not a normal TV station. It is a propaganda tool, well built, you know, well paid. And as far as I understand, you know, alongside with military and interior forces, those are protected items in the budget because Putin knows that he needs his propaganda machine, and we should confront him on this turf as well. Thank you.

Senator JOHNSON. We have unilateral desires when it comes to providing information and the truth. President Saakashvili, any final thoughts?

Mr. SAAKASHVILI. Yes. Yes. Senator, I wanted to thank you for this hearing. We have now live feed to many Ukrainian television channels. It is a country of more than 40 million people, and I think many of them will be watching what is being said in the U.S. Congress and this committee. More than that, you know, I mean, in Georgia it is being watched. In Moldova it is being watched. In Georgia they have the Saakashvili presidential library, and actually after midnight. And I was just told by my assistant there is a full hall. They are assembled watching it live on television. And that can tell you people come and showing up so late at night watching or trying to watch this together, what kind of impact these kind events have in our part of world.

And that is one part of it. So the other part of it is that Putin never made secret that he is not after Poroshenko or after any of this. He is after the United States. He has said it publicly many times. He has depicted his confrontation with the United States. So even if some elements in the United States would not want to be part of it, but from Putin's point of view they are, and he is striking at the U.S. interests.

So from that standpoint, it is very important that with all the moral support the people have been getting, especially from this building and from your committee and from you personally, Senator, they now finally get also the ultimate decisions because those decisions are going to make huge—will have besides, like very concrete changes on the ground, huge moral boosting effect because in these kind of confrontations, it is very important, I know it from our experience, to know that you are on the right side.

So, again, thank you, Senator, for being on the right side today together with other members of the committee. And thank you for all your support, and your impact, and your contribution.

Senator JOHNSON. Well, again, I want to thank all of the witnesses for your time, your thoughtful testimony, as Dr. Blank said, for telling the truth, and for just fighting for freedom.

The record will remain open until the close of business on March 11, one week from today, for questions for the record.

Senator JOHNSON. This hearing is adjourned.

[Whereupon, at 4:28 p.m., the hearing was adjourned.]

ADDITIONAL MATERIAL SUBMITTED FOR THE RECORD

PHOTOS OF RUSSIA'S INVASION SUBMITTED BY SENATOR RON JOHNSON

Facts of Russian military equipment and weapons presence on the territory of Ukraine

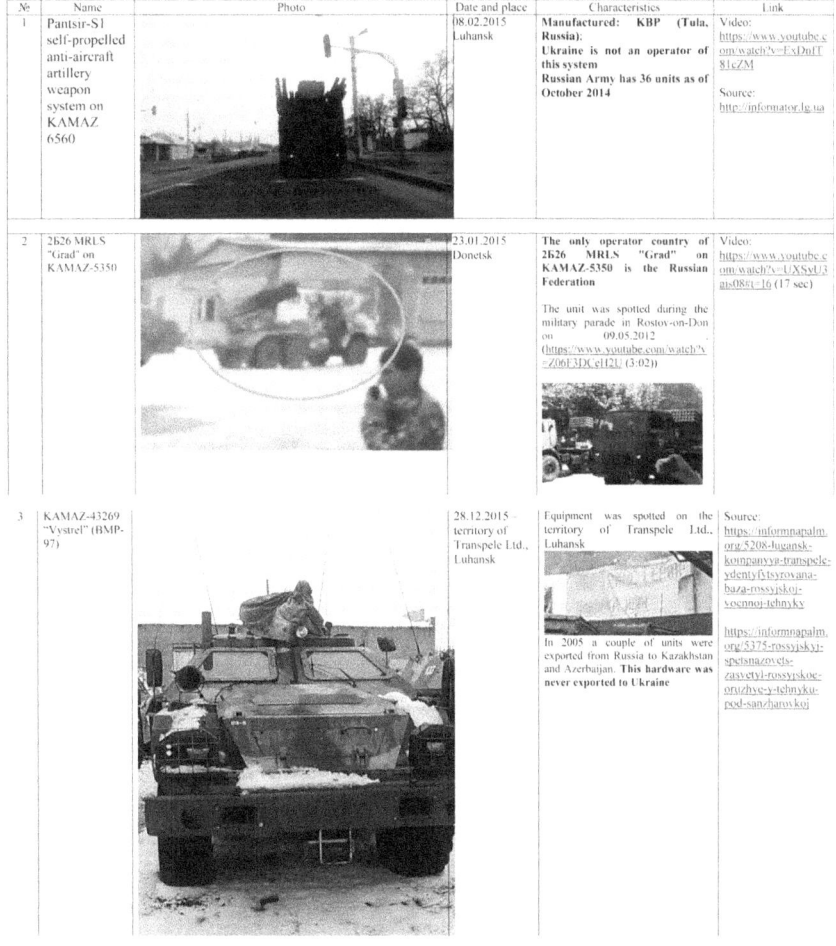

4	Body armor and helmet from the Russian infantry combat system "Ratnik"		Summer 2014 Donetsk region **Body armor and helmet found near the destroyed "DPR" equipment**	**Ratnik** (Russian, *Ратник*; Warrior) is a Russian infantry combat system.	Link: https://www.youtube.com/watch?v=PJTOBQ_R9Sw&feature=youtu.be
5	Special assault rifle AS "Val"		12.01.2015 Donetsk, Central market	**Russian Special Forces are equipped with AS "Val"**	Video: https://www.youtube.com/watch?v=SjOHLDaLAk9t=26 Source: https://informnapalm.org/4793-gary-putler-y-dary-smerty
6	MRLS 9K58 «Smerch» - Russian multiple rocket launch system	Photo 1	Photo 1: 22.01.2015 Makiivka, Donetsk region. Photo 2: 10.02.2015 Makiivka, Lenina Str. Donetsk region.	MRLS 9K58 «Smerch» - Soviet and Russian multiple rocket launch system, caliber – 300mm.	Video: https://www.youtube.com/watch?v=gLm-GjIt.9K8 https://www.youtube.com/watch?v=AcoOptQ8J3oA

Photo 2

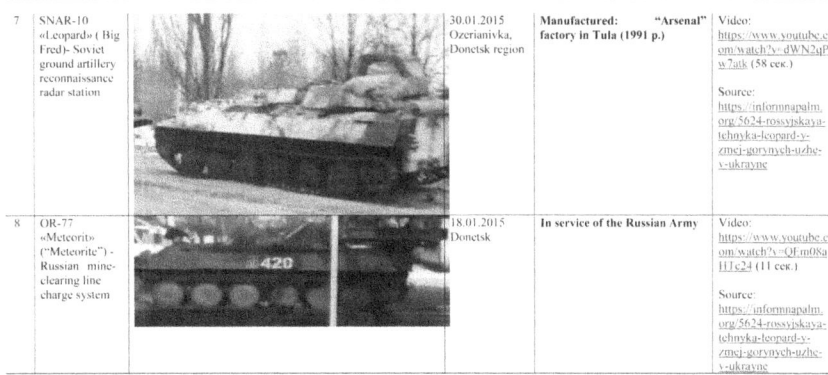

| 7 | SNAR-10 «Leopard» (Big Fred)- Soviet ground artillery reconnaissance radar station | | 30.01.2015 Ozerianivka, Donetsk region | Manufactured: "Arsenal" factory in Tula (1991 р.) | Video: https://www.youtube.com/watch?v=dWN2qPw7atk (58 сек.)

Source: https://informnapalm.org/5624-rossyjskaya-tehnyka-leopard-y-zmej-gorynych-uzhe-v-ukrayne |
| 8 | OR-77 «Meteorit» ("Meteorite") - Russian mine-clearing line charge system | | 18.01.2015 Donetsk | In service of the Russian Army | Video: https://www.youtube.com/watch?x=QFm08aH1c24 (11 сек.)

Source: https://informnapalm.org/5624-rossyjskaya-tehnyka-leopard-y-zmej-gorynych-uzhe-v-ukrayne |

| 9 | Kord-12.7 mm heavy machine gun |  | 08-09.2014 Donetsk region | **Designed:** 1997; **Produced since:** 2006 At present serial production establish, machine gun **is in service by the Armed Forces of the Russian Federation** | Video: https://www.youtube.com/watch?v=_9RPhdjoZlhU (5:02) Source: https://informnapalm.org/3703-russian-kord-in-donbass |
| 10 | Thermobaric (TBG-7), Foto 1 and fragmentation (OG-7), Foto 2 munitions for RPG-7 grenade launcher | Photo 1  Photo 2 | 31.08.2014 Donetsk region | **TBG-7V «Tanin» / 7P33** (Foto 1); Type of warhead: thermobaric; **OG-7V «Oskolok» / 7P50** (Foto 2); Type of warhead: fragmentation; | Video: https://www.youtube.com/watch?v=FAoA7s4eoug (1:45) https://www.youtube.com/watch?v=azjFpgiWwlk (1:19) Source: https://informnapalm.org/4793-garry-putler-y-dary-smerty |